Some Slaveholders

and

Their Slaves
Union Parish, Louisiana
1839-1865

Harry F. Dill and William Simpson

HERITAGE BOOKS
2007

HERITAGE BOOKS
AN IMPRINT OF HERITAGE BOOKS, INC.

Books, CDs, and more—Worldwide

For our listing of thousands of titles see our website
at
www.HeritageBooks.com

Published 2007 by
HERITAGE BOOKS, INC.
Publishing Division
65 East Main Street
Westminster, Maryland 21157-5026

Other books by Harry F. Dill:

Marriages & Deaths from The Caucasian, Shreveport, Louisiana, 1903-1913
Appointments of Postmasters in Louisiana, 12 January 1827-28 December 1892

International Standard Book Number: 978-0-7884-0617-1

TABLE OF CONTENTS

PREFACE

Union Parish, located in the north center part of Louisiana, was established on 13 March 1839 from a portion of Ouachita Parish by an act of the legislature to create a new judicial district. It derived its name from the sentiment of the time--"liberty and union, now and forever, one and inseparable" (from a speech by Daniel Webster).

The 1860 population census shows that persons born in Louisiana were outnumbered by settlers who came from other states during the early- and mid-1800s. For the most part, the new arrivals were farmers who soon discovered that the land was suitable for growing a variety of crops, such as cotton, potatoes, beans, peas, and sugar cane. (From its beginning, Union Parish has remained a cotton parish.) Milch cows, cattle, wild horses, swine, and sheep for wool were in abundance.

Natural gas, lumbering, and manufacturing of wood products have contributed to the economy of the parish for many decades. Lumbering and natural gas today account for a major portion of the monetary worth of the parish, as does agriculture. Union Parish is also a center for growing and distribution of watermelons.

Farmerville, the parish seat, was named after a prominent family of the area. William Wood Farmer, who served as lieutenant governor from 1852 to 1853, died in New Orleans of yellow fever on 29 October 1854; his remains were removed to Farmerville Cemetery on 15 January 1855.

The courthouse has extensive volumes of original documents that date from the founding of the parish. All of these papers are in excellent condition. It was from these sources, and from population censuses, telling as they do, a poignant, dramatic story of people who lived in those days of slavery, that the authors have gleaned information for this book.

v

The purpose of this work is to provide a handy reference for anyone, black or white, seeking ancestors who came to, or were born in, and who lived in Union Parish during the period covered by this book.

We hope that many of our readers will locate their long-lost progenitors in these pages.

POPULATION CENSUS,
SCHEDULE 2.--SLAVE INHABITANTS,
UNION PARISH, LOUISIANA,
18 JUNE 1860-6 AUGUST 1860

The form used nationwide by enumerators to record data for the 1860 Population Census, Schedule 2.--Slave Inhabitants, has but meager information for identifying a person's ancestors; names of slaveholders, and total number of slaves by sex, age, and color are the few clues provided.

To the complete list of slaveholders of Union Parish, Louisiana, the authors have added elements from the 1860 Population Census, Schedule 1.--Free Inhabitants, that are not part of Schedule 2.--age, sex, occupation, place of birth, and place of residence in Union Parish. These additional elements could prove useful to anyone seeking ancestors who might have resided in Union Parish at the time the 1860 census enumerations were made.

(Most documents refer to slaves usually by given names only; however, some complete slave names are recorded in this book (see Slave Index).)

In some cases, complete spellings of slaveholders' names could not be determined from Schedule 2.--Slave Inhabitants, initials only having been recorded. However, by cross-referencing the index to the 1860 Schedule 1.--Free Inhabitants, the 1860 Schedule 2.--Slave Inhabitants, conveyances (slave deeds), and successions, the authors expanded many initials into actual given names. Since the Census schedules often showed initials only, cross-referencing offers many opportunities for researchers to identify their ancestors, by having full names available.

Many persons who did not appear on Schedule 2.--Slave Inhabitants, but who owned slaves before and after the 1860 enumerations, are included in this book. Their identity as slaveholders is reflected in slave deeds and in successions.

Name, Residence in 1860	Age	Sex	Occupation	Place of Birth
John A. Hammock Shiloh	34	M	Farmer	GA
Evans Gaskill Shiloh	76	M	Blacksmith	VA
W. W. Brown Shiloh	25	M	Teacher, Common School	SC
A. D. Gaskill Shiloh	54	M	M. D.	TN
A. Wade Shiloh	37	M	Farmer	VA
James Thomas Wade Shiloh	26	M	Overseer	VA
P. T. Moore Shiloh	29	M	Farmer	AL
William Bennett Shiloh	43	M	Farmer	NC
Thomas J. Moore Shiloh	23	M	Farmer	AL
Richard C. Pullum Shiloh	48	M	Farmer	SC
John Welden Shiloh	35	M	Farmer	AL
Daniel Lowery Shiloh	33	M	Farmer	AL
A. W. Harris Shiloh	48	M	Farmer	GA
J. M. Bennett Shiloh	70	F	Farmer	NC
Nancy C. Smith Shiloh	42	F	Farmer	TN
Adline Bevil Shiloh	41	F	Farmer	SC
P. J. Shackelford Shiloh	60	M	Farmer	GA
Thomas Gray Shiloh	24	M	Farmer	GA

Name	Age	Sex	Occupation	Birthplace
Mary Heard Shiloh	33	F	Farmer	GA
Henry Plyant Shiloh	55	M	Farmer	SC
Leroy Findley Shiloh	47	M	Farmer	GA
William Hopkins Shiloh	53	M	Farmer	GA
James M. Crawford Shiloh	65	M	Farmer	GA
Thomas Pearson Shiloh	36	M	Farmer	SC
John A. Leach Shiloh	34	M	Farmer	SC
Solomon Feazel Shiloh	49	M	Farmer	LA
J. C. B. White Shiloh	33	M	Farmer	KY
D. M. Goodger Cherry Ridge	27	M	Farmer	AL
Martha Goodger Cherry Ridge	44	F	Farmer	SC
G. W. Lockwood Springhill	15	M	None	LA
G. W. Murphy Springhill	39	M	Farmer	AR
David Redden Shiloh	32	M	Farmer	KY
E. P. Bolton GA Shiloh	50	M	Teacher, Languages	
Joseph Shaw Shiloh	35	M	Farmer	MS
Henry W. Hamilton Shiloh	48	M	Farmer	SC
George W. Tabor Shiloh	27	M	Farmer	MS
James S. Sutton Shiloh	12	M	None	AR

4

Name	Age	Sex	Occupation	Birthplace
George W. Moore Shiloh	34	M	Farmer	AL
Jesse G. Fuller Shiloh	42	M	Farmer	AL
James E. Goodwin Shiloh	31	M	Farmer	AL
F. Barnett Shiloh	65	M	Farmer	SC
W. P. Smith Shiloh	33	M	Farmer	GA
Asa Coker Shiloh	37	M	Farmer	SC
James H. Johnson Shiloh	56	M	Farmer	GA
James Martin Hendrick Shiloh	35	M	Farmer	GA
John B. Tubb Shiloh	37	M	Farmer	AL
Benjamin Tubb Shiloh	33	M	Farmer	AL
J. R. Clark Shiloh	40	M	M. D.	MD
John A. Barham Shiloh	25	M	Farmer	GA
James Edwards Shiloh	48	M	Farmer	GA
Ruffin G. Pleasant Shiloh	43	M	Merchant	NC
William C. Heard Shiloh	50	M	Farmer	GA
G. W. Cox Shiloh	44	M	Farmer	NC
Nancy Edmunds Shiloh	49	F	Farmer	GA
William Patton Shiloh	32	M	Farmer	GA
Thomas Robinson Shiloh	42	M	Farmer	GA
William Tubb	58	M	Farmer	TN

Shiloh				
Ellen McClelland	55	F	Farmer	GA
Shiloh				
George W. Lowery	30	M	Farmer	AL
Shiloh				
Thomas Lowery	31	M	Farmer	AL
Shiloh				
James Lowery	45	M	Farmer	AL
Shiloh				
Harriett Tubb	52	F	Farmer	GA
Shiloh				
John S. Hammock	59	M	Farmer	GA
Shiloh				
D. M. Wright	45	M	Farmer	GA
Shiloh				
Cynthia Fuller	37	F	Farmer	AL
Shiloh				
A. J. Fuller	25	M	Farmer	GA
Shiloh				
John G. Wright Sr	52	M	Farmer	GA
Shiloh				
John E. Norris	23	M	Farmer	AL
Shiloh				
John G. Wright Jr	22	M	Farmer	AL
Shiloh				
Eliza Williams	35	F	Farmer	AL
Shiloh				
S. S. Heard	55	M	Farmer	GA
Shiloh				
Callaway Green	26	M	Farmer	AL
Shiloh				
C. J. Henry	45	M	Farmer	SC
Shiloh				
C. Marion Fuller	32	M	Farmer	AL
Shiloh				
W. N. Autry	26	M	Farmer	AL
Shiloh				
J. S. Lovelady	49	M	Farmer	TN
Shiloh				

J. M. Pinkard	38	M	Farmer	AL
Shiloh				
J. F. Mitchell	43	F	Farmer	SC
Shiloh				
Joseph H. Morrow	31	M	Farmer	AL
Shiloh				
Absalom Autry	58	M	Farmer	NC
Shiloh				
Mary Mobley	9	F	None	SC
Shiloh				
William Moore	26	M	Farmer	AL
Shiloh				
J. W. Wright	28	M	Farmer	AL
Shiloh				
James M. Tatum	49	M	Farmer	GA
Shiloh				
Thomas H. Wright	58	M	Farmer	GA
Shiloh				
John Green	58	M	Farmer	NC
Shiloh				
D. W. Green	34	M	Farmer	AL
Shiloh				
Wiley Cook	46	M	Farmer	SC
Shiloh				
Louis Leggin	42	M	Farmer	GA
Shiloh				
James G. Leggin	64	M	Farmer	VA
Shiloh				
Russell Huffman	40	M	Farmer	SC
Shiloh				
Charles R. Lawrence	34	M	Farmer	AL
Shiloh				
John B. Green Jr	28	M	Farmer	AL
Downsville				
William M. Lawrence	42	M	Farmer	GA
Downsville				
W. M. Gill	47	M	Farmer	GA
Downsville				
John C. Colvin	31	M	Farmer	SC

Name	Age	Sex	Occupation	State
Downsville				
A. Beck	50	M	Farmer	SC
Downsville				
H. Barmoore	50	M	Farmer	SC
Downsville				
A. M. Brothers	21	M	Farmer	NC
Downsville				
John B. Mitchell	34	M	Farmer	TN
Downsville				
Nancy Davis	50	F	Farmer	GA
Downsville				
William O. Jones	26	M	Farmer	NC
Downsville				
Wiley White	40	M	Farmer	AL
Downsville				
Eliza Hobday	53	F	Farmer	NC
Downsville				
Benjamin J. Hobday	21	M	Farmer	AL
Downsville				
Jeanette Hobday	18	F	None	AL
Downsville				
Archibald D. McDuffie	38	M	Farmer	NC
Downsville				
John M. Ford	31	M	Farmer	AL
Downsville				
George A. Stinson	42	M	Farmer	GA
Downsville				
D. McNaughton	53	M	Farmer	GA
Downsville				
Louis Rush	64	M	Farmer	GA
Downsville				
Hiram Brewster	64	M	Farmer	GA
Downsville				
John J. Hester	34	M	Farmer	AL
Downsville				
William G. Mattox	40	M	Farmer	GA
Downsville				
America Martin	27	M	Farmer	AL
Cherry Ridge				

James McCown	57	M	Farmer	MS
Downsville				
John Carter	53	M	Farmer	GA
Downsville				
James Hays	52	M	Farmer	GA
Downsville				
William Brewster	29	M	Farmer	AL
Downsville				
W. J. Smith	29	M	Farmer	GA
Downsville				
William S. Norris	48	M	Farmer	KY
Downsville				

P. 559, 1860 Population Census, Schedule 1.-Free Inhabitants, has these entries:

William S. Norris	48	M	Farmer	born KY
In Household:				
Bright Baker (Mulatto)	15	M	Farm Laborer	AL
Jack Baker (Black)	15	M	Farm Laborer	AL
Mary Baker (Black)	12	F	Farm Laborer	AL

William White	48	M	Farmer	GA
Downsville				
R. R. Roberts	27	M	Teacher, Common School	SC
Downsville				
John T. Tidwell	38	M	Farmer	SC
Downsville				
W. C. Bush	40	M	Farmer	GA
Downsville				
John Williams	55	M	Farmer	GA
Downsville				
G. P. Runnells	30	M	Farmer	GA
Downsville				
Elias Taylor	44	M	Farmer	GA
Downsville				
William J. Wilhite	57	M	Farmer	NC
Downsville				
Austin Honeycutt	42	M	Farmer	LA
Downsville				

9

Stacy Keener	46	F	Farmer	GA
Downsville				
Thomas Sellers	45	M	Farmer	NC
Downsville				
Benjamin C. Ellis	50	M	Farmer	NC
Downsville				
S. T. Hester	39	M	Farmer	AL
Downsville				
John Hester	31	M	Farmer	AL
Downsville				
G. W. Reynolds	48	M	Farmer	NY
Downsville				
Francis McCormick	59	M	Farmer	SC
Downsville				
C. W. Hodge	45	M	Farmer	GA
Downsville				
D. Morris	60	F	Housekeeper	SC
Downsville				
H. C. Spellers	44	M	Farmer	SC
Downsville				
J. T. Hester	67	M	Farmer	NC
Downsville				
Nancy Stanley	35	F	Farmer	AL
Downsville				
Benjamin F. Farmer	36	M	Farmer	LA
Downsville				
James C. Manning	54	M	Farmer	SC
Downsville				
J. G. Culp	46	M	Farmer	SC
Downsville				
L. C. Callaway	55	M	Farmer	GA
Downsville				
James Augustus Manning	25	M	Farmer	AL
Downsville				
John C. Callaway	26	M	Farmer	MS
Downsville				
J. E. Woodard	30	M	M. D.	NC
Downsville				
P. Wilhite	50	M	Merchant	NC

Downsville				
W. B. Wallace	39	M	Farmer	GA
Downsville				
C. Buchanan	35	M	Farmer	AL
Downsville				
Charles C. Raily	43	M	Farmer	GA
Downsville				
A. McFarland	49	M	Farmer	NC
Downsville				
Mary C. Ellis	42	F	Farmer	MS
Downsville				
William Pipes	49	M	Farmer	MS
Downsville				
P. Feazel	65	M	Farmer	TN
Downsville				
J. O. Feazel	60	M	Farmer	TN
Downsville				
John Culbertson	69	M	Farmer	GA
Downsville				
William H. Culbertson	48	M	Farmer	GA
Downsville				
L. T. Culbertson	30	M	Farmer	AL
Downsville				
Jackson Dickerson	34	M	Farmer	AL
Downsville				
N. S. Crawford	28	M	Farmer	SC
Downsville				
Thomas Seals	45	M	Farmer	SC
Downsville				
Thomas Cox	50	M	Farmer	GA
Downsville				
W. H. Crawford	51	M	Farmer	GA
Downsville				
James King	40	M	Farmer	GA
Downsville				
Charles P. King	26	M	Farmer	GA
Downsville				
William Albritton	38	M	Farmer	NC
Downsville				

David Stewart	24	M	Farmer	LA
Downsville				
John Shields	35	M	Farmer	LA
Downsville				
George W. Sims	45	M	Hotel Keeper	GA
Downsville				
F. L. Cook	28	M	M. D.	AL
Downsville				
Simpson W. Ramsey	35	M	Farmer	AL
Downsville				
C. H. Griffin	20	M	Farmer	GA
Downsville				
Henry P. Anderson	46	M	Farmer	TN
Downsville				
John L. Barrett	35	M	Attorney	VT
Farmerville				
Nancy Lewis	48	F	Housekeeper	LA
Farmerville				
Reddick P. Bruton	53	M	Farmer	NC
Farmerville				
W. H. Carson	40	M	Farmer	KY
Farmerville				
H. M. Carson	37	M	Merchant	KY
Farmerville				
George Rossiter	61	M	Farmer	MA
Farmerville				
John Archer	32	M	Farmer	AL
Farmerville				
Lazarus Brunner	30	F	Merchant	Germany
Farmerville				
J. Shlenker	23	F	Merchant	Germany
Downsville				
Allan M. Callaway	31	M	Sheriff	AL
Farmerville				
J. W. Vines	45	M	Mechanic	SC
Spearsville				
James M. Underwood	31	M	Farmer	AL
Farmerville				
A. T. Bayless	40	F	Housekeeper	KY

Downsville				
John E. Baker	55	M	Farmer	AL
Farmerville				
Cullen H. Edwards	38	M	Farmer	VA
Downsville				
J. E. Tremble	26	M	Teacher, Languages	PA
Farmerville				
William McDuffie	30	M	Mechanic	NC
Farmerville				
George A. Kilgore	40	M	Farmer	GA
Farmerville				
Edward B. Windes	38	M	Farmer	MS
Farmerville				

(The census enumerator indicated that a 100-year-old female slave named "Timpy" was owned by Edward B. Windes)

Benjamin F. Dillard	40	M	M. D.	VA
Farmerville				
David Vines	87	M	Farmer	SC
Farmerville				
S. C. Lee	34	M	Merchant	AL
Farmerville				
William Cleaton Carr	50	M	M. D.	GA
Farmerville				
John Odom	48	M	Farmer	SC
Farmerville				
William H. Glasson	36	M	Farmer	GA
Farmerville				
Henry Regenburg	40	M	Attorney	Denmark
Farmerville				
F. H. Carr	28	M	Farmer	England
Farmerville				
William A. Dean	38	M	Barkeeper	NC
Farmerville				
William Claiborne Smith	30	M	Court Recorder	AL
Farmerville				
T. S. Thompson	60	M	Farmer	VA
Farmerville				
James Jones	36	M	Farmer	MS
Farmerville				

Thomas Gilbert	20	M	Farmer	AL
Spearsville				
James R. Gilbert	23	M	Farmer	AL
Spearsville				
Jesse E. Pearson	25	M	Farmer	AL
Farmerville				
John Harvey	44	M	Farmer	TN
Farmerville				
William A. Darby	41	M	Farmer	NC
Farmerville				
Charles H. Gilbert	49	M	Farmer	AL
Farmerville				
Ansel Kitchens	38	M	Farmer	GA
Farmerville				
Frank Rabon	41	M	Farmer	GA
Farmerville				
Joseph Pardue	40	M	Farmer	AL
Farmerville				
William M. Beard	66	M	Farmer	NC
Farmerville				
R. Edwards	38	M	Farmer	VA
Marion				
James Montgomery	22	M	Farmer	AL
Marion				
C. Edwards	45	M	Farmer	GA
Farmerville				
Mary L. Stewart	46	F	Farmer	LA
Shiloh				
Liberty K. Thomas	48	M	Farmer	SC
Marion				
Uriah Bass	51	M	Farmer	NC
Marion				
Elizabeth Brantley	36	F	Farmer	MS
Marion				
George Jessup	44	M	Farmer	NY
Marion				
A. Bates	45	M	Farmer	SC
Marion				
Henry B. Muse	50	M	Farmer	SC

Location	Name	Age	Sex	Occupation	State
Shiloh	J. B. Sheppard	35	M	Farmer	AL
Cherry Ridge	George Little	41	M	Farmer	GA
Cherry Ridge	M. T. Simmons	44	M	Farmer	GA
Cherry Ridge	J. B. Short	52	M	Farmer	LA
Cherry Ridge	W. M. Wasom	45	M	Farmer	TN
Cherry Ridge	John Rabon	27	M	Farmer	AL
Cherry Ridge	William Rabon	47	M	Farmer	GA
Cherry Ridge	Sarah Dean	21	F	Farmer	NC
Cherry Ridge	George Tubb	24	M	Farmer	MS
Cherry Ridge	Joseph G. King	29	M	Farmer	KY
Cherry Ridge	E. Lee	58	M	Farmer	NC
Cherry Ridge	John Gray	58	M	Farmer	GA
Cherry Ridge	Allen Futch	40	M	Farmer	AL
Cherry Ridge	Jesse Odom	42	M	Farmer	SC
Cherry Ridge	Benjamin M. Tubb	40	M	Farmer	AL
Cherry Ridge	D. Rabon	71	M	Farmer	SC
Cherry Ridge	John Phelps	41	M	Farmer	SC
Cherry Ridge	F. B. Glasson	41	M	Farmer	SC
Cherry Ridge	Nancy Taylor	33	F	Farmer	AL
Cherry Ridge					

John T. Mathis	41	M	Farmer	AL
Cherry Ridge				
John F. Burford	71	M	Farmer	AL
Cherry Ridge				
Elias Farris	63	M	Farmer	SC
Cherry Ridge				
Jeremiah S. Doumas	40	M	Farmer	GA
Cherry Ridge				
Joseph R. McGough	10	M	None	LA
Farmerville				
M. Hendrick	49	M	Farmer	GA
Cherry Ridge				
Wesley W. Lockwood	45	M	Farmer	GA
Cherry Ridge				
H. L. Buckley	61	M	Farmer	VA
Springhill				
J. T. B. Andrews	35	M	Farmer	NC
Springhill				
Duncan D. Dawkins	40	M	Farmer	NC
Springhill				
John Holloway	41	M	Farmer	AL
Springhill				
J. G. Bilberry	32	M	Farmer	AL
Springhill				
A. Pistole	37	M	Farmer	TN
Springhill				
John S. Watkins	32	M	Farmer	GA
Springhill				
E. Jones	32	M	Farmer	AL
Springhill				
John M. White	20	M	Farmer	AL
Springhill				
James A. Creath	41	M	Farmer	VA
Springhill				
J. B. L. Robinson	43	M	Farmer	NC
Springhill				
J. B. Eckles	58	M	Farmer	VA
Springhill				
M. E. Daniel	37	M	Farmer	NC

Name	Age	Sex	Occupation	State
Springhill				
E. O. G. Andrews	35	M	M. D.	NC
Springhill				
J. W. Caskey	36	M	Farmer	SC
Springhill				
C. C. Clark	32	M	Farmer	MS
Springhill				
H. K. Elkins	38	M	Farmer	NC
Springhill				
Thomas Kilgore	51	M	Farmer	GA
Cherry Ridge				
Ashley Nelson	46	M	Farmer	GA
Spearsville				
J. P. Harrell	27	M	Farmer	NC
Spearsville				
C. C. McDaniel	47	M	Farmer	NC
Spearsville				
Daniel J. Abbott	40	M	Farmer	AL
Spearsville				
Charles C. Dildy	41	M	Farmer	NC
Spearsville				
A. Patterson	60	M	Farmer	NC
Spearsville				
Y. K. Light	40	M	Farmer	GA
Spearsville				
James M. Williams	28	M	Farmer	AL
Spearsville				
W. L. Dearing	60	M	Farmer	VA
Spearsville				
F. M. Carroll	43	M	Farmer	AL
Spearsville				
John Gray	40	M	Farmer	AL
Spearsville				
D. C. M. Post	30	M	Farmer	AL
Spearsville				
Thomas J. Griffin	47	M	Farmer	SC
Spearsville				
J. H. Farrow	38	M	Farmer	AL
Spearsville				

William Farrow	45	M	Farmer	AL
Spearsville				
R. Brazel	60	M	Farmer	GA
Spearsville				
A. Stansil	60	M	Farmer	NC
Farmerville				
A. T. Hayes	50	M	Farmer	SC
Farmerville				
W. C. Hall	38	M	Farmer	GA
Farmerville				
John Steel	55	M	Farmer	SC
Farmerville				
J. M. Lee	30	M	Farmer	AL
Farmerville				
Alexander M. Taylor	54	M	Farmer	GA
Farmerville				
J. H. Gulley	45	M	Farmer	NC
Cherry Ridge				
Daniel Joseph Abbott	35	M	Farmer	AL
Spearsville				
W. J. Goyne	45	M	Farmer	GA
Farmerville				
W. A. Wooley	22	M	Farmer	AL
Spearsville				
J. R. Goyne	30	M	Merchant	GA
Farmerville				
H. C. Barron	56	M	Farmer	GA
Spearsville				
Nancy Ford	31	F	Farmer	AL
Marion				
S. M. Brooks	46	M	M. D.	PA
Spearsville				
M. D. Lee	62	M	Farmer	NC
Spearsville				
William H. McGough	34	M	Farmer	AL
Farmerville				
Sarah Taylor	10	F	None	LA
Downsville				
J. G. Taylor	30	M	Farmer	AL

Name	Age	Sex	Occupation	Birthplace
Farmerville				
John Taylor	56	M	Farmer	GA
Farmerville				
William R. Albritton	34	M	Farmer	AL
Farmerville				
Eli Owens	53	M	Farmer	GA
Farmerville				
George W. Albritton	38	M	Farmer	NC
Farmerville				
John Aulds	25	M	Farmer	AL
Farmerville				
Davis Goyne	30	M	Farmer	GA
Farmerville				
Henry Funderburk	73	M	Farmer	SC
Farmerville				
James Cargel	30	M	Farmer	LA
Farmerville				
James Colston	45	M	Farmer	AL
Farmerville				
J. M. Terry	57	M	Farmer	SC
Farmerville				
David Ward	53	M	Farmer	GA
Farmerville				
William L. Gulley Sr	50	M	Farmer	AL
Farmerville				
William Ham	58	M	Farmer	VA
Farmerville				
Hillary Hub Ham	32	M	Farmer	GA
Farmerville				
R. J. Ham	30	M	Farmer	GA
Farmerville				
M. Little	40	M	Farmer	GA
Farmerville				
L. A. Doaty	23	M	Farmer	TN
Farmerville				
B. F. Low	23	M	Farmer	MS
Farmerville				
M. A. Gilbert	24	F	Farmer	GA
Farmerville				

Pinkney Odom	40	M	Farmer	SC
Farmerville				
S. P. Ford	43	F	Farmer	NC
Farmerville				
S. H. Griffin	26	M	Farmer	GA
Farmerville				
H. C. Barron	27	M	Farmer	GA
Spearsville				
O. B. Hill	52	M	Merchant	NH
Spearsville				
David M. Jameson	40	M	M. D.	PA
Spearsville				
James Barron	60	M	Farmer	GA
Spearsville				
Nealy Vines	50	M	Farmer	SC
Spearsville				
T. J. Gilbert	52	M	Farmer	GA
Spearsville				
James F. McAdams	35	M	Farmer	AL
Spearsville				
Isaac Williams	29	M	Farmer	GA
Spearsville				
William Anderson	46	M	Farmer	TN
Spearsville				
John Galbreath	40	M	Teacher,	NC
Spearsville			Common School	
Louis Rabon	50	M	Farmer	MS
Spearsville				
Jeremiah Hays	50	M	Farmer	GA
Spearsville				
William T. Thompson	57	M	Farmer	KY
Spearsville				
Rebecca Mathis	48	F	Farmer	SC
Spearsville				
William Lowe	35	M	Farmer	AL
Spearsville				
G. W. Clayton	58	M	Farmer	SC
Spearsville				
J. C. Runnells	40	M	Farmer	SC

Spearsville A. Lee	45	M	Farmer	AL
Spearsville William Pearson	30	M	Farmer	AL
Spearsville W. J. Pickle	33	M	Merchant	TN
Spearsville John M. Godley	34	M	Farmer	GA
Springhill John P. Everett	34	M	Farmer	AL
Springhill R. F. Farrow	30	M	Farmer	AL
Springhill Thomas M. Everett	36	M	Farmer	AL
Marion John W. Wood	60	M	Farmer	GA
Marion James McFadin	37	M	Farmer	NC
Marion Samuel J. Larkin	60	M	Farmer	NC
Marion Miles W. Goldsby	60	M	Farmer	GA
Marion John Trailer	53	M	M. D.	AL
Marion John Taylor	30	M	Farmer	AL
Farmerville E. R. Puckett	33	F	Farmer	LA
Marion Jordan Taylor	22	M	Teacher, Common School	AL
Marion S. E. Trailer	25	M	Farmer	AL
Marion Matilda A. Masterson	47	F	Farmer	GA
Marion Britten Honeycutt	28	M	Farmer	LA
Marion S. B. Thomas	61	M	Farmer	SC
Marion				

21

T. J. Stewart	40	M	Farmer	LA
Marion				
John Crow	46	M	Farmer	GA
Marion				
J. W. Walker	38	M	Farmer	SC
Marion				
James M. Turner	49	M	Farmer	MS
Marion				
James Jeter	64	M	Farmer	SC
Marion				
J. M. Spencer	35	M	Farmer	AL
Marion				
W. J. Smith	29	M	Farmer	AL
Spearsville				
Green B. Alford	34	M	Farmer	GA
Marion				
D. Shaw	70	M	Farmer	NC
Marion				
Abel Robb	41	M	Farmer	AL
Marion				
S. W. Phillips	30	M	Farmer	VA
Marion				
Courtney L. Norman	40	M	Farmer	AL
Marion				
G. Cabril	39	M	Farmer	LA
Marion				
Charles M. Absent	48	M	Farmer	SC
Marion				
J. G. Hollis	57	M	Farmer	SC
Marion				
J. B. Ivey	37	M	Farmer	AL
Marion				
D. D. Dawson	40	M	Farmer	NC
Farmerville				
Benjamin Ford	53	M	Farmer	GA
Marion				
R. J. Sims	30	M	Farmer	GA
Marion				
J. A. Stringer	51	M	Farmer	SC

Location	Name	Age	Sex	Occupation	State
Marion	E. Stripling	38	F	Farmer	AL
Marion	J. S. Stripling	40	M	Farmer	GA
Marion	E. Parker	23	M	Farmer	MS
Marion	S. Chapman	53	M	Farmer	NC
Marion	John T. Smith	70	M	Farmer	GA
Marion	L. C. Reppond	70	M	Farmer	GA
Marion	Benjamin F. George	28	M	Farmer	AL
Marion	B. B. Thomas	23	M	Farmer	AL
Marion	Gabriel N. Benson	22	M	Farmer	AL
Marion	Felix G. Hargis	26	M	Attorney	LA
Marion	Martha Ann George	31	F	Farmer	AL
Marion	L. P. Loper	41	M	Farmer	SC
Marion	L. M. Powell	37	M	Farmer	AL
Marion	C. T. Powell	29	M	Farmer	AL
Marion	James Wallis	53	M	Farmer	AL
Spearsville	W. A. Wallas	44	M	Farmer	NC
Marion	W. W. Walker	35	M	Farmer	TN
Marion	S. L. Robinson	37	M	Farmer	SC
Marion	D. J. Tucker	42	M	Farmer	SC
Marion					

Arthur Stripling	72	M	Farmer	NC
Marion				
W. D. M. Bruton	34	M	M. D.	NC
Marion				
John B. Robertson	34	M	Farmer	VA
Springhill				
John E. Green	42	M	Farmer	NC
Marion				
James Moore	60	M	Farmer	SC
Marion				
E. B. Bilberry	32	M	Farmer	AL
Marion				
Mary Honeycutt	60	F	Farmer	TN
Marion				
L. Cooper	27	M	Farmer	MS
Marion				
C. M. Cooper	25	M	Farmer	MS
Marion				
T. S. Cooper	37	M	Farmer	MS
Marion				
William Bird	55	M	Farmer	GA
Marion				
Thomas W. Anderson	22	M	Farmer	GA
Marion				
Don Pedro Acquilla Cook	57	M	Farmer	GA
Marion				
W. E. Davis	33	M	Farmer	GA
Marion				
T. L. Davis	37	M	Timberman	AL
Marion				
T. J. Tatum	27	M	Farmer	AL
Marion				

ABSTRACTS OF SUCCESSIONS, 1839-1865

Union Parish was formed from a portion of Ouchita Parish on 13 March 1839. In some parishes, a system of estate administration called probate was used. However, estate administration and other actions are found in successions, rather than in probates, from 1839 to the present in Union Parish.

Some actions resolved by successions were:

--Administration of estates of deceased persons

--Emancipation (a petition was submitted to the judicial court, by a person under legal age of 21, male or female, giving reasons why early majority was sought)

--Tutorship of minor children

--Guardianship

--Tutorship or guardianship of incompetents

--Disposition of real and personal property, the latter category including slaves

Many succession processes included several of these actions at the same time. A male under 21 could petition the judicial court for "emancipation," be granted his request, and could then ask to be appointed as estate administrator, tutor, or guardian. He could also cause inventories to be made, and could monitor the auction of slaves and other property.

The judicial court, which alone had the authority to grant or deny petitions, sometimes directed that property be sold to satisfy indebtedness. When no indebtedness was involved, the court ruled that personal property and real estate be sold, and the proceeds divided among the heirs. The court could also mandate that lots be drawn by heirs, who then became owners of slaves, other personal property, and real estate.

Family meetings were often held, to determine actions, such as appointment of tutors, partition of land, selection of slaves for auction, and setting up lots of slaves to be drawn by family members. Each family meeting action had to be approved by the judicial court.

Book H, P 1   Succession of Lorenzo A. Griffin, June 1839, died 14 Mar 1839. Mentions widow, Mariah Griffin; daughter, Julia Ann Temperence Griffin, 4; sons, John William Griffin, 2, and William Lorenzo Addison Griffin, 20 months. Slave: Eliza, 20.

Book H, P 162   Succession based upon petition by Thomas W. Smith, September 1839. Mentions Thomas Smith Heard, deceased, and Heard's daughter, Emily. Smith requested legal documents be processed to show he gave to Emily L. Traylor, his adopted child, certain slaves. The judicial court honored his request and, on 1 Jan 1840, Emily L. Traylor became legal owner of following slaves, no ages shown: Maria, Harriett, Celia, Francis, Nancy, Green, Susan, Ellen, and Porter.

Book W, P 6   Succession of Susan Henry, January 1841, died 4 Oct 1840. Mentions husband, Daniel Colvin Sr, daughter, Elizabeth Johnson, wife of Job Johnson, and father, James Henry, deceased. Slaves: Charity, 35, and children, Rachel, 11, Burr, 9 months, Melinda, 7, Sarah, 5, Jane, 3, and James, 3 months; Shadrach, 25, Alex, 23, and Sun, a girl, 13, sold at auction to Daniel Colvin Sr; Lucy, 16, Sophia, 22, and Bill, 20, sold to Jeptha Colvin; Ann, 24, and children, Mary, 18 months, and Ann, 2 months, sold to Daniel Colvin Jr.

Book A-1, P 212   Succession of Mary Alexander Henry, June 1841, died 17 Apr 1841. Mentions husband, James Henry, sons, John F. Henry and James Henry II. John F. Henry purchased slaves Jack, 15, and Sing, female, no age shown. Clementine H. Richardson purchased Mima, 50.

Book W, P 51   Succession of Jesse Cooper, March 1842, died January 1841. Mentions widow, Anna Cooper, daughter, Martha Jane Cooper, sons, William O. Cooper, Thomas F. Cooper, Lexington Cooper, and Marshal Colombus Cooper. Slaves: Lucinda, 35, Wiley, 7, George, 8, Peggy, 1, Robb, 20, and Frank, 14. The court ruled that all slaves were the property of Anna Cooper.

Book A, P 217   Succession of Anny Hall, November 1842, died 1841. Mentions husband, John Hall, died in Alabama, Permelia Kennedy, William C. Hall, and James Hall. Slaves sold at auction were

Lucinda, also called "Cyndy" (no age shown), and children, Harriett, 6, Joanna, 4, to John Hall; Eady, 14, to James Hall; Joe, 30, to William C. Hall.

Book A-1, P 403 Succession of William D. May, April 1843, died 29 Aug 1841. Mentions widow, Catherine Guice May, brother, John May, James F. May, Henry May, Stephen D. May, Daniel May, and Phillip May. Peter, "a small negro boy," was sold to Benjamin May. Property owned in partnership by William May, deceased, and John May, purchased by John May: Delcey, 20, and children, Margaret, 3, and Nancy, 9 months; Delphey, 25, and children, Ann, Thomas, and Sarah, all under 10; Tom, 60, his wife, Fanny, 38; Charles, 39, Dave, 25, Henry, 30, and Harriett, 10. Purchased by Catherine Guice May were Simon, 40, and Charity, 40.

Book A-1, P 477 Succession of Susannah Farmer, November 1843, died 21 Oct 1843. Mentions sons, W. W. Farmer and John N. Farmer; Sarah E. Feazel, Leah Farmer, Rachel Farmer, Benjamin F. Farmer, and James McCown, son of Daniel McCown, former husband of Susannah Farmer. Sold at auction were Eliza, no age shown, and children, Humphrey, Joshua, Aaron, and Lonsey, all under 10, and Dandrige, 35, and Nicey, 40, sold to W. L. Payne. King, 60, Clarissa, 40, Hugh, 44, and Isaac, 12, sold to W. W. Farmer. Nelson, 29, sold to James Malawin. Willis, 22, sold to John Farmer. Huldah, no age shown, and children, Jacks, Edmond, and Arthur (no ages shown), and Dennis, 18, sold to William Wilhite. Mariah, 28, and children, Chastity and Nelson, both under ten, sold to Solomon Feazel. Hagar, female, 13, sold to Rachel Sterling. Chany, 30, and children, Marshal, Harriett, Alsey, Hannah, and Forrest, all under 10, sold to Rachel Farmer. Penelope, 40, Reuben, 11, and Joseph, 4, sold to Thomas J. Wilhite.

Book A-1, P 554 Sucession of William E. Fuller, March 1844, died 7 Feb 1843. Mentions mother, Mary Fuller, and father, Jesse Fuller. Slave Peter, 12, was purchased by Isaac C. Mays.

Book A-1, P 275 Succession of Dr. William C. Carr, June 1844, died 14 May 1844. Mentions daughter, Susan Carr, 14, son, Allen Carr, 17, and brother, Allen C. Carr. Slaves: Mariah, 30, and children, Charity, 8, Nelson, 3, and Nancy, 2 months. Diannah, 20, and children, Emaline, 4, Jefferson, 3, and Green, 1. Tempey, female, 60, Sarah Ann, 17, and Jenny, 25, and daughter, Mariah, 9.

Book A-1, P 640   Succession of George W. Griffin, March 1844, date of death not shown. Mentions widow, Louisa S. Griffin, deceased; minor children, Sidney H. Griffin, Mary Ann Griffin, and Simpson W. Ramsey, tutor and administrator. Lots were drawn by Simpson W. Ramsey on behalf of minor children to establish ownership of slaves. Lot #1, for Sidney H. Griffin: Jesse, 40, Gilbert, 8, Abram, 6, Henry, 17, Chany, 18, and infant; Sukey, female, 40, Big Sally, no age shown, and child, Frances, 4; Catherine, 10, and Stephen, 4. Lot #2, for Mary Ann Griffin: Philip, 35, Wade, 17, Willis, 12, Charles, 6, Mary, 4, Cynthia, 60, Isabel, 6, North, 10, and Little Sally, no age shown, and son, Mose, 2.

Book C, P 102   Succession of George Felix Heard, September 1845, date of death not shown. Mentions widow, Emily Smith Traylor Heard, deceased, son, Thomas Smith Heard, died 7 July 1845, and Josiah C. Traylor, administrator. (At death, Thomas Smith Heard was 4 years and 9 months old.) Slaves: Sealy, 30, and daughter, Lucinda, no age shown; Jefferson, 3, Porter, 13, Jane, 7, Harrison, 24, Nancy, 11, James, 2, Mariah, 13, Frances, 11, Ellen, 6, Peter, 54, and Harriett, 10.

Book C, P 93   Succession of Timothy Crane, November 1845, died 28 Aug 1845. Mentions Edward Crane. Also mentions that no heirs survived. Slaves: Winney, 30, and son, Andy, 6.

Book A-2, P 527   Succession of Armstead Norman, January 1846, died 6 Apr 1841. Mentions daughter, Lavina Norman, sons, Calvin Norman and Courtney Norman. The court ruled that the following slaves be sold at auction to satisfy debts: Filler and son, no ages shown, purchased by Sylvester Norman. Abner, Easter and Delila, no ages shown, purchased by Sarah Norman. Jake, no age shown, purchased by Frances Norman.

Book H, P 88   Succession of Roland Manning, February 1846, died 27 Feb 1844. Mentions widow, Elizabeth Manning, now wife of John Odom, William T. H. E. Manning and Harriett Manning. Slaves:

Chany, 40, and son, Joe, 9 months; Charlotte, 28, and daughter, Mira, 6 months, purchased by David Hendrick. (Succession indicated that Mira died in 1846). No disposition shown for Harry, 9, Jefferson, 20 months, Emily, 5, Chany, 36, Nelson, 12, and Nathan, 26.

Book A-2, P 546 Succession of Andrew Parker, March 1846, died 4 Dec 1843. Mentions father, John Parker, sister, Sarah Parker, wife of George Anderson. Slaves, Dick, Bill, Alfred, and Harry, no ages shown, purchased by W. I. Q. Baker on 6 Jan 1847.

Book C, P 127 Succession of Nancy Courtney Bird, March 1846, died 15 Apr 1845. Mentions husband, William Bird, deceased, and son, Ezra Bird, who purchased Jake, 38, at auction.

Book C, P 303 Succession of Oliver H. P. Windes, August 1847, died 11 Mar 1847. Mentions brothers, Edward B. Windes and Robert W. Windes. Slaves: Hamilton, 27, Martha, 18, and son, Henry, no age shown; Jemima, 13, and Mary, 15.

Book C, P 379 Succession of Benjamin Harrison, September 1847, died April 1847. Mentions widow, Jemima Ann Ratliffe Harrison, now wife of James M. Crawford, son, William Allen Harrison, and daughter, Sarah Harrison, minors. Slaves of the estate were purchased by Jemima Harrison Crawford and her husband James M. Crawford: Fanny, 40, and daughter, Fay, 17; an infant, no sex or age shown; Rhodo, female, 17, Little Dave, 23; and Woodley, 50. No ages were shown for Phillis, Wiley, Cinna, George, Rachel, Old Dave, Lucinda, and Easter and son, Nelson.

Book 26, P 183 Succession of George Holloway, September 1847, died 26 Jan 1846. Mentions widow, Jane Holloway, sons, William L. Holloway and James L. Holloway. Slaves: Mariah, 25, and daughter, Melissa, 2; Dorcas, 20, and children, Nolia, 1, and Isaac, 2 weeks; Jacob, 30, Sam, 27, John, 19, Alexander, 3, Charity, 35, Stephen, 30, Alcy, 36, Nelson, 27, March, 25, Jacob, 4, Landers, 40, and Joe, Tom, and Caroline, no ages shown.

Book C, P 244 Succession of Nancy Marion Evans, December 1847, died 19 Jul 1847. Mentions husband, George M. Savage. Based upon her will, the court declared George M. Savage owner of the following slaves: Winney, 30, and children, Hillyard, 11 months, March, 2, Godfrey, 7, and Harry, 12; Cloy, 45, and children, Melissa, 8, and Lucy, 6; Sawyer, 45, Phillip (runaway), 34, Stipney, male, 45, Derry, 50, Old Phillip, no age shown, Little Silva, 22, and Big Rachel, 40; Leah, 28, and children, Prince Albert, 7, and Bedford, 2; Charlo, female, 25, Louisa, 14, Margaret, 14, Selvey, female, 50, Ester, 25, Caroline, 8, Mary Ann, 12, John, 30, Priss, female, 10, Dick, 44, Bob, 45, Alfred, 25, Cipio, male, 34, Tom, 45, and Ceasor, 60.

Book A-2, P 230 Succession of Camilla Lianda Killam, March 1849, died 7 Mar 1847. Mentions mother, Eliza Foy Killam, now wife of Burrell H. Jones, father, James Killam, deceased, and brother, James Warren Killam, 4. Slaves (no ages shown): Rose, Ned, Malina, Frances, Allen, Jim, Jack, Nancy, Lavina (died in 1847), and Esther and son, Peter North, born in 1847.

Book A-1, P 423 Succession of Benjamin E. Davis, March 1848, died 26 Jun 1846. Mentions wife, Matilda Holaday, wife #1; sons by Matilda: Benjamin F. Davis, Thomas I. Davis, and Columbus C. Davis; daughter by Matilda, Mary Frances Davis; wife #2, Malinda Kelly, sons by Malinda, John K. Davis and Walter A. Davis. Slaves: Maria, 25, and children, Martha, 6, Mary, 3, Henry, 2, and Sam, infant; Doc, 17, Primas, 50, Daniel, 43, and Raney, female, 14.

Book C, P 366 Succession of Jesse Brantley, June 1849, died May 1849. Mentions wife, Elizabeth Brantley, and Thomas Brantley. Slaves: Everett, Derry, John, Mirah, Peggy, and Mariah and children, Emily, Pegge, Martha, and Marunna (no ages shown).

Book C, P 392 Succession of Elijah Annisett, November 1849, died 1849. Mentions brother, Jesse Annisett, daughters, Charlotte Annisett, Eliza D. Annisett, Martha Annisett, and Virginia Annisett, and son, Andrew Annisett. Slaves: Patience, no age shown, and child, not named; Jim, Dan, Harrison, and Wesley (no ages shown).

Book A-2, P 572 Succession of Moses Pearson, December 1849, died 1849. Mentions widow, Eleanor Pearson, sons, Davis

Pearson, William, and Jesse Pearson. Slaves (no ages shown): Winney A, Morrison, Peggy, and children, Mary, Kizy, girl, Manerva, Rachel, Jane, John, Lize, and Lafayett; Friday, Will, Sampson, Sally, Allen, and Frank; Lucy, and children, Alex, Sam, Sarah, Rose, Adeline, Nancy, and Tabbett, boy.

Book A, P 547 Succession of Elisha Parker, July 1852, died 6 Oct 1848. Mentions widow, Sally Parker, and minor children, Asa Parker and William Parker. On inventory of personal property and identified as a slave was Phillis, no age shown.

Book A, P 369 Succession of William T. H. Manning, February 1853. Mentions widow, Mary Manning, now wife of Benjamin P. Cook. The judicial court ordered that the following slaves be sold at public auction: Harry, 18, was purchased by William Ham; Major, 11, was purchased by John Odom. (Succession indicated that both boys had run away, but were later apprehended in Rusk County, Texas, and returned to Union Parish.)

Book A, P 3 Succession of John D. Rimes, December 1853, died March 1853. Mentions widow, Louisa C. Rimes, daughter, Cinderella Rimes, sons, William L. Rimes, Francis L. Rimes, and Thomas W. Rimes. Wilson, a slave boy, 14 was purchased by Silas Phillips at public auction.

Book A-2, P 100 Succession of Phoebe Hendrick, September 1854, died 8 Mar 1852. Mentions husband, David Hendrick, and son, David Hendrick Jr. Slaves: Dicy, 10, Sharper, 51, Henry, 5, Manerva, 2, Charles, 33, and Juda, 28.

Book A, P 391 Succession of James Matthews, non compos mentis, October 1854. Mentions sister, Mary Ann Mason, tutrix, guardian, and administratrix. Mary Ann petitioned the court for authority to remove her brother, James Matthews, and personal property, including slaves, from Union Parish to Adams County, Mississippi. Her request was granted 9 Apr 1855. (Names of slaves not shown.)

Book A-2, P 385 Succession of Mary Jane Masterson, October 1854, died 4 Sep 1852. Mentions husband, Marshall Masterson, deceased, mother, Matilda Masterson, daughters, Matilda Cole, Mary Turner, Prudence Graves, and Louisa Gresham. Slaves: Turner, 17, purchased by McDual Bilberry.

Book A-3, P 305 Succession of Mary P. Ward, January 1856, died 1855. Mentions George W. Everett, administrator. Slaves: Winney, 15, and child, no name, age, or sex shown, purchased by A. W. Johnson. W. D. M. Bruton purchased Isaac, 38.

Book A-2, P 163 Succession of Thomas Ivey, April 1856, died 27 May 1849. Mentions widow, Nancy Ivey. Slaves: Abram, 35, wife Peggy, and children, Jenny, 8, John, 6, Legrand, 4, and infant; Aaron, 14, Ellen, 10, Jacob, no age shown, George, 16, and Betty, 17, and son, Solomon, no age shown. (All slaves were purchased at auction by Henry Regenburg, attorney.)

Book A-3, P 84 Succession of John Rogers, July 1856, died 1856. Slaves: Caroline and children, no names or ages shown, purchased at auction by William A. Doty. Harriett, no age shown, purchased by John Gaskins. Mariah, Marion, George, Green, Thomas, Margaret, and Mary Jane, no ages shown, purchased by Permelia Morris.

Book A-2, P 569 Succession of Dorothy Payne, May 1858. Mentions father, Daniel Payne, and daughter, Delaware Jones, only surviving child, wife of William O. Jones. Slaves: Catherine, 17, John, 20, and Malinda, 30.

Book A, P 429 Succession of John D. McLaurin, September 1858. Mentions D. K. McLaurin. Slaves: Jacob, his wife Lidea, and children, Nelly, July, Margaret, and Easter, no ages shown; Little Aggy, and son, Solomon, no ages shown.

Book A-3, P 114 Succession of Sylvanus Shepherd, February 1859, died 1858. Mentions James B. Shepherd, and W. C. Carr, administrator. Slaves: Bitty, 42, and children, Kate, 11, Dinah, 9, and Andy, 16, purchased by James B. Shepherd. Grandison, 12, purchased by A. W. McCormick. Jane, 25, and children, Angelina, 4, Stephen, 3, and Susan, 13, purchased by William C. Carr.

Book A-3, P 205 Succession of David G. Stewart, September 1859, died 1 Sep 1859. Mentions widow, Mary L. Stewart, sons, Washington W. Stewart, and Jonathan B. Stewart, daughter, Nancy E. Stewart Stanley. Slave, Abram, no age shown, purchased by Nancy Stanley.

Book A-1, P 583 Succession of William T. Gilbert, January 1860. Mentions widow, Mary Ann Gilbert, and Sidney H. Gilbert. Slaves: Mary, 20, and son, John, 2; Susetter, 40, and children, Emaline, 9, Sarah, 5, and Laura, 3; Mary Ann, 17, and infant, Frances; Jim, 31, Mose, 50, Henry, 22, Wade, 23, Mary Ann, 21, Mose, 14, Anderson, 10, and Sally, 20.

Book A-1, P 456 Succession of Rosco Edmonds, March 1860. Mentions widow, Nancy Edmonds, and William J. Edmonds. Slaves: Milly, 28, and children, Adaline, 6, Betsey, 4, and Dilcy, 1; Charlotte, 28, Garner, 24, Wyatt, 16, Sermantha, 25, Henry, 14, and Cynthia, 11.

Book A, P 72 Succession of Joseph M. Heard, February 1860, died 21 Dec 1859. Mentions widow, Mary Heard. On inventory was Joe, a slave, 50 years old.

Book E, P 354 Succession of Susan Ann Mixon Honeycutt, June 1860. Mentions Austin Honeycutt, Eliza Honeycutt, and Jesse Honeycutt. Slaves: Caroline, 25, and children, Louisa, 7, Ringo, 5, and Chase, 3; Hannah, 24, and children, Jesse, 5, and Sarah, infant; Peter, 68, Mary, 19.

Book A-3, P 88 Succession of Dr. Lucien F. Rowland, June 1860. Mentions widow, Sarah H. Bryant, and Mary E. Bryant. Declared property of Mary E. Bryant by the court were Willis and Lorenzo, no ages shown.

Book A-3, P 321 Succession of Job M. Williams, August 1860, died 8 Jul 1860. Mentions daughter, Rachel C. Williams, and son, John C. Williams. Slaves: Nancy, 40, and children, Aleck, 6, and daughter, Friday, 1; Caroline, 15, Martha, 14, and Warren, 13.

Book A-3, P 229   Succession of William Sutton, July 1860. Mentions sons, James D. Sutton and John S. Sutton, and daughter, Sara Jane Sutton. Slaves: Olly, no age shown, and daughter, Harriett, 5; Lorsden, 35, Crease, female, 26, and Louisa, 26.

Book A-1, P 123   Succession of John A. Bayless, December 1860. Mentions widow, Nancy D. Bayless, and daughter, Martha Bayless. Purchased at auction by Nancy D. Bayless were slaves Moses, 15, Sally, 8, and Henry, no age shown.

Book E, P 67   Succession of Washington L. George, September 1860, died June 1857. Mentions widow, Martha Ann George, and sons, Washington E. George, and Benjamin F. George, and daughter, Eliza George. Slaves: Lucinda, 34, and children, Robert, 8, Frank, 6, and Doc, 3; Mary, 34, and children, Elizabeth, 9, and Fanny, 7; Johnston, 30, Ellen, 33, Rachel, 14, John, 18, and Martha, 24.

Book A-1, P 426   Succession of Martha F. Davis, January 1861, died March 1860. Mentions husband, William E. Davis. Slaves: Henry, 35, Jane, 35, and children, Lucy, 5, and Noah, 2; Mary, 13, Sarah, 11, Jim, 20, and Sandy and son, Jim, 4.

Book E, P 427   Succession of Daniel B. Acree, February 1861, died 31 Oct 1860. Mentions widow, Rachel Acree Farmer, now wife of Benjamin F. Farmer. Slaves: Martha, 25, and children, James, 6, Nelson, 4, Ellen, 3, Harriett, 2, and Henry, infant; Hannah, 24, Chany, 50, and George, 18.

Book A, P 282   Succession of James H. Carson, February 1861, died 10 Dec 1860. Mentions widow, Elizabeth Carson, and W. H. Carson. The court ruled that slaves be sold at auction: John, 21, and Joe, 28, purchased by James M. Underwood. Washington, 28, purchased by J. R. Thompson. Edward, 32, purchased by John West. Wallace, 33, purchased by William H. Glasson. Rachel, 36, purchased by Moses S. Carson. Caroline, 38, purchased by Cullen H. Edwards. Lewis, 30, purchased by David M. Jameson.

Book A-2, P 502   Succession of Ashley S. Nelson, March 1861. Mentions widow, Nancy Ann Matilda Nelson. Slaves: Nelly, 34, and children, Daniel, 11, Jack, 8, Emily, 6, and Elbut, male, 4 months; Martha, 50, and children, Ann, 6, and Julia, 2; Henry, 65, Eli, 14, John, 18, Elbut, 38, William, 26, Isaac, 12, Jacob, 21, Dely, 22, Ephriam, 30, and Susan, 11.

Book A-2, P 44   Succession of John Harvey, April 1861. Mentions widow, Elizabeth Harvey. Slaves: Bicea, female, 45, and Joe, 55.

Book E, P 167   Succession of Henry Funderburk, April 1861, died 22 Dec 1860. Mentions widow, Deborah A. Funderburk, now wife of Joel P. Kelly. Slaves: Eliza, no age shown, and daughter, Amanda, 7 months; Rachel, 27, and children, George, 9, Elizabeth, 5, and Eliza, 18 months; Jiney and son, Ben, 6 months; Lubuty, 16, Ned, 25, Madison, 14, Bob, 12, and Emily, 10.

Book E, P 74   Succession of Thomas E. Graham, May 1861. Mentions widow, Margaret J. Graham, now wife of James Augustus Manning, son, George R. Graham, Isabella Mattox, wife #1 of Thomas B. Graham, now wife of William B. Mattox. At a family meeting it was agreed to draw lots for ownership of slaves. Lot #1, Isaac, 50, drawn by John A. Graham. Lot #2, Gilley, 30, and infant, Nelly, drawn by Margaret J. Manning. Lot #3, Henry, 13, drawn by Miss Evander M. Graham. Lot #4, Eliza, 11 drawn by Isabella A. Mattox. Lot #5, Laura, 5, and Randal, 7, drawn by Archibald D. McDuffie, tutor, on behalf of George R. Graham, minor.

Book A-2, P 379   Succession of James A. Martin, June 1861, died 21 May 1860. Mentions sons, James Martin and Wiley Martin, daughters, Martha Martin and Netty Martin. Slaves: Daniel, 30, and Bob, 20.

Book E, P 220   Succession of Thomas Van Hook, June 1861. Mentions widow, Maria E. Van Hook, daughters, Mary Van Hook, and Charity Van Hook, and sons, Wade Van Hook, Allen Van Hook, and Jackson Van Hook. Slaves: Ellen, and sons John and Littleton, no ages shown.

Book E, P 282 Succession of Alexander M. Taylor, July 1861. Mentions widow, Winfred Taylor Mathis. Slaves: Colara, 30, and children, Sam, 9, Charley, 6, and Alvin, 3; Charlotte, 18, and infant, age and sex not shown; Violette, 17, and infant, Miller, age not shown; Rachel, 50, and son, Anderson, 6; Eliza, 21, and son, Bob, 1; Hannah, 15, Buck, 23, Kitty, 26, Jack, 55, Amanda, 26, Sandy, 16, Penny, 25, Abe, 21, Joe, 11, Alvin, 3, Edmund, 57, Harry, 16, Jim, 20, Frank, 35, Aaron, 19, George, 12, Gil, 9, Amy, 60, Dick, 42, and Ann, 19.

Book A-1, P 593 Succession of John M. Godley, July 1861, died 6 Jan 1860. Mentions widow, Martha A. Godley, now wife of James B. Godley, daughters, Mary A. Godley and Elizabeth Godley, and son, Columbus Godley. Slaves: Mary, 35, and children, Elizabeth, 9, and Fanny, 7; Will, 35, Charity, 5, Wash, 9, Agnes, 7, Mariah, 12, Henry, 16, and Emily, 14.

Book A-3, P 226 Succession of George W. Stripling, August 1861, died April 1859. Mentions Arthur Stripling, administrator. Slaves: Lucinda, 23, and children, Sally, 4, Ben, 2, and Parthenia, 5 months.

Book A-1, P 235 Succession of John F. Burford, August 1861. Mentions widow, Sarah A. Burford, sons, John F. Burford Jr, Robert Burford, and William Burford. At a family meeting, lots were drawn for ownership of slaves, the action approved by the judicial court. Lot #1, Louisa, 17, and daughter, Judy, no age shown; John, 37, Vina, 10, Lenoc, 7, and Amanda, 10, drawn by Elizabeth Burford McGough, wife of W. S. McGough. Lot #2, Floid, 37, Hannah, 20, Henry, 4, Sally, 18, and George, 12, drawn by Robert Burford. Lot #3, London, 26, Cook, 14, Thomas, 8, Mehalah, 14, and Winney, 10, drawn by John F. Burford Jr. Lot #4, Sabre, and children, Stephen, no age shown, and Clinsa, 2; Ben, 38, Easter, 21, and Benjamin, 6, drawn by Sarah A. Burford.

Book A-2, P 529 Succession of Courtney L. Norman, October 1861, died 20 Sep 1861. Mentions widow, Martha H. Norman. Slaves: Harrison, 21, Parthenia, 17, William, 13, and Julia, 19.

Book A-2, P 413 Succession of Catherine M. McCormick, November 1861. Mentions husband, Francis McCormick, daughter, Julia A. McCormick, and sons, Benjamin McCormick and George L. McCormick. Slave: Charles, 39.

Book A-1, P 602 Succession of James M. Goodwin, January 1862, died in the military service 24 Sep 1861. Mentions widow, Martha A. Goodwin. Slaves: Paul, 56, Emily, 23, and Celia, 18.

Book A-1, P 82 Succession of John W. Baker, February 1862, "died in Confederate Army Service." Mentions John E. Baker. No slaves mentioned. (A John Baker, of Farmerville, is on slave inhabitants census as owning slaves.)

Book A-1, P 580 Succession of Charles S. Gilbert, February 1862. Mentions sons, R. M. Gilbert, Thomas F. Gilbert, and William Darby, administrator. Sold at public auction were following slaves: Phebe, 25, and children, Malipa, 6, Mariah, 4, and Ailsey, purchased by A.C. Darby. Patience, 22, and children, Dread, 5, and Ann, 4, purchased by Liberty K. Thomas. Amanda and child, purchased by James R. Gilbert. Peter, 35, purchased by R. M. Gilbert. Amanda, 15, purchased by William A. Darby. Sipp, male, 30, purchased by Pinkney Odom. Dick, 35, purchased by G. W. Clayton. Dred, 23, Hester, 6, and Ropetta, 4, purchased by John Archer. Clarea, 13, Anthony, 10, and Sarah, 20, purchased by B. F. Lowe. Emiline, 10, purchased by Mrs. E. A. Rossiter. Rachel, 4, purchased by Thomas F. Gilbert.

Book E, P 385 Succession of John B. Tubb, February 1862, died 21 Dec 1861. Mentions widow, Elizabeth Tubb, now wife of William Tubb. Slaves: Daniel, 35, Susan, 29, and Aly, girl, 4.

Book A-2, P 317 Succession of Elizabeth Lowery, June 1862. Mentions James Lowery and Daniel Lowery, daughter, Georgia A. Lowery. Slaves: Hannah, no age shown, and children, Dorcas, 5,

Eliza, 3, and Jasbelia, 1; Chany, and children, Willie, 3 and Mary Jane, 1; Harry, 60, and Andy, 35.

Book E, P 571 Succession of Nancy J. Creath, July 1862, died February 1862. Mentions husband, James A. Creath. Slaves: Patience, 24, and children, Viny, 9, Mary, 7, and Caroline, 2; Emily, 24 and children, Ellen, 8, Frances, 5, and Alfred, 3; Bird, 23, Jim, 45, Cacey, female, 35, Fred, 19, Nace, 15, Bicea, female, 35, and Angeline, 35.

Book A-1, P 521 Succession of Solomon Feazel, August 1862. Mentions Philip Feazel, John Feazel and Isiah S. Feazel. Slaves: Martha, 22, and children, Charity, 7, and Ben, 2; Margaret, 28, and children, Jerry, 8, Aron, 4, and Ann, 2; Gilbert, 23, Tom, 65, Patty, 20, Bill, 19, Andy, 23, and Jack, 27.

Book A-2, P 72 Succession of Joseph M. Heard, August 1862. Mentions widow, Mary Heard, and son, S. L. Heard. Slave: Joe, 54.

Book A-1, P 409 Succession of Stephen R. Crow, September 1862, "died in Confederate Army Service, April 1862." Mentions widow, Lucinda Crow, and son, John Crow. Slave: Matilda, 28.

Book A-2, P 594 Succession of Gabriel R. Plummer, October 1862, "departed this life April 1862 while serving his country in the Army." Mentions widow, Jone (sic) Plummer, now wife of M. W. Goldsby, and son, Earnest Plummer. Slaves: Margaret, 22, and children, Edward, 5, and Alice, 4; Orleana, 28, and children, Jim, 8, Lewis, 6, and Elias, 4; Wily, 62, Darcas, 51, Bob, 65, Roan, 14, Lapley, girl, 9, Abley, boy, 4, Mary, 65, Bob, 17, Silas, 25, Bill, 12, Lizzie, 18, Sophia, 17, Jerry, 7, and Willey, 9.

Book A-2, P 389 Succession of Matilda A. Masterson, November 1862. Mentions daughters, Mary Jane Masterson and Louisa Masterson. Slaves: Mary, no age shown, and children, Esquire, 9, Amanda, 6, George, 4, Reuben, 2, and infant.

Book A-2, P 411 Succession of James M. McClelland, November 1862, died 21 Jun 1862. Mentions widow, Ellen

McClelland, Francis McClelland, and Frances J. Smith, former wife of James M. McClelland, now wife of Robert J. Heath. Slave: Harris, 19.

Book A-3, P 261   Succession of George W. Tabor, January 1863. Mentions widow, Mary W. Edmonds Tabor, and John Burrell Tabor. Slaves: Ed, 25, and Charlott, 15.

Book A-2, P 24   Succession of Felix G. Hargis, March 1863. Mentions widow, Elizabeth A. Hargis, daughter, Ella Hargis, and son, Felix G Hargis Jr. Slave: Ruben, 24.

Book A-1, P 96   Succession of John A. Barham, May 1863, died 15 March 1862. Mentions widow, Mary C. Clark, daughter, Martha Barham, and sons, William F. Barham and John F. Barham. Slaves: Katy, 35, Albert, 10, and Joe, 25.

Book A-3, P 90   Succession of Elizabeth Ann Rossiter, August 1863, died July 1863. Mentions husband, George Rossiter, daughter, Harriett D. Rossiter, wife of Robert C. Webb Jr, son, Jefferson B. Rossiter, minor, George W. Aulds, John J. Aulds, and William A. Aulds, sons of Adaline (Rossiter) Aulds, deceased. At a family meeting, lots were drawn for ownership of slaves. Lot #1, Green, 37, Jim, 8, and Jane, 8, drawn by George M. M. Rossiter. Lot #2, Revs, 26, and Em, 14, drawn by George Rossiter. Lot #3, Beth, 30, and children, Lucy, 3, Ann, 5, and Charles, 8, drawn by Amanda J. Waters. Lot #4, Mariah, 24, and children, Wiley, 12, and Mary, 1, drawn by Jefferson B. Rossiter. Lot #5, Violet, 19, Wright, 10, and Jerry, 11, drawn by Harriett Webb. Lot #6, Rose, 13, Ellen, 12, and Burell, 15, drawn by William W. Aulds.

Book A-1, P 436   Succession of William A. Dean, September 1863. Mentions sons, John Dean and Jesse Dean. Slave: Betty, 60.

Book A-1, P 581   Succession of James R. Gilbert, December 1863, "died about November 1863 in the Army." Mentions R. M. Gilbert and William A. Darby, administrator. The court ordered slaves be sold at auction to satisfy debts: Amanda, 25, and children, Sally, 5, Louisa, 3, and Julian, 2, purchased by Jeff Fuller. Jordan, 35, purchased by William A. Darby.

Book A-1, P 644 Succession of Sidney H. Griffin, April 1864, "died in the service of the country on or about 27 Jun 1863." Mentions widow, Catherine E. Griffin, also referred to as Catherine West, and daughters, Ada Griffin and Ellen Griffin. Slaves: Winney, 55, and children, George, 9, and Ann, 7; Patsey, 19, and son, Jence, 2; Frank and her son, John, 2; Merrel, male, 34, Harriett, 17, Rocky, female, 15, Gilbert, 26, Stephen, 22, Lucky, female, 33, Abe, 24, Benton, 18, Matilda, 16, Susan, 15, Elijah, 9, Mary, 6, and Sallie, 65.

Book A-2, P 460 Succession of S. David Mims, March 1864, died March 1862. Mentions minor sons, R. L. C. Mims and S. D. Mims Jr. Slaves: Ann, 46, and children, Spencer, 7, Delia, 4, and Fanny, 2; Harriett, 38, and children, Ross, 7, West, 9, and Mary, 12; Caroline, 22 and children, Ellen, 6, William, 4, and Arch, 3; Mander, female, 5, Charlie, 18, Marion, infant, Zelpha, 17, Sarah, 12, Aaron, 48, Bill, 33, Glasco, 17, Alfred, 20, Pompy, male, 50, Eli, 15, Charles 32, and Celler and her infant, Jeff, no ages shown.

Book A-1, P 473 Succession of Benjamin F. Farmer, March 1864, "died July 1862 in the service of the Confederate States Army." Mentions widow, Mary Farmer. Slaves: George, 35, and Aaron, 17.

Book A-2, P 246 Succession of Charles P. King, March 1864, "died in service with the army." Mentions Joseph G. King, sons William King and Henry King, and daughter, Mary King. Only two slaves, Manerva, 21, and son, Frank, 10 months, were on the personal property inventory.

Book A-3, P 332 Succession of Edward B. Windes, March 1864. Mentions Elizabeth Windes, now wife of Robert W. Futch. Slaves: Emaline, 23, and infant daughter, Jefalonia; Martha, 16, and son, Elias, 7 months; Andrew, 41, Moses, 14, Joe, 43, Frank, 33, Jasper, 21, Hamilton, 53, Mariah, 38, Ann, 28, Henry, 13, and Dorcas, 23.

Book E, P 642. Succession of John M. Ford, September 1864, "died in the Army." No slaves mentioned. (A John M. Ford, of Downsville, is on slave inhabitants census as owning slaves.)

Book A-3, P 351   Succession of John E. Wright, October 1864. Mentions widow, Sarah Ann Wright, daughter, Sarah Ann Wright Tatum, sons, Thomas R. Wright, John Wright, and Owen Wright. Slaves: Chaney, and children, Mary, 3, and Jim, 18 months; Bittie, 18, and daughter, Lucinda, 4 months; Eda, 40, Emily, 13, Malina, 40, Dearing, 45, George, 16, Squire, 18, Lotta, 25, Abraham, 38, Howard, 25, Sam, 17, Frank, 16, Rose, 23, Clara, 40, Jesse, 12, Bill, 16, Gilbert, 12, Cenia, 10, Ben, 32, Henry, 20, Dennis, 14, Ellick, 14, and Sarah, 45.

Book A-2, P 329 Succession of Larken W. Lowery, September 1864, died 29 Aug 1862. Mentions widow, Martha A. Edmonds, sons, Thomas Lowery and George Lowery. Slaves: Malina, 35, and children, Harry, 9, Charley, 6, Sandy, 3 months, Ashack, 4, and Rachel, 2; Milly, 15, Hanna, 27, and children, Dorcas, 5, Eliza, 3, and Esbella, 1; Chaney, 20, Isaac, 47, Harry, 62, Andy, 33, Dick, 32, Peter, 12, and Willis, 4.

Book E, P 437   Succession of Cullen H. Edwards, October 1864, "died in service of Confederate States Army, April 1862." Mentions widow, Mary Jane Edmonds. Slave: Caroline, 38.

Book E, P 201   Succession of Gabriel N. Benson, December 1864, died 5 Sep 1862. Mentions Benjamin F. George, administrator. The judicial court ordered the following slaves be sold to satisfy debts: Martha, 25, and children, Bill, 2, Nett, 5, and Marion, infant; Elisha, 22, and Isham, 30 purchased by Wiley J. Hammock. Dinah/Diannah, 35, and children, Amanda, 6, and Frances, 7, purchased by C. Donaghay. Wiley, 71 and wife Mary, 65; Bob, 62, and Silas, 35, purchased by Gabriel R. Plummer. Jesse, 25, purchased by William L. Glasson. Peter, 10, purchased by James Jeter. Cynthia, 18, purchased by Daniel Shaw. Clinsa, 24, Reuben, 24, and Ellick, 19, purchased by Elias George.

Book E, P 726   Succession of Joseph H. Morrow, December 1864, died 20 Jul 1864. Mentions widow, Mary Henry, also referred to as Nancy Morrow, now wife of Charles Henry, sons, Charles Morrow and William Morrow, and daughter, Alabama Morrow. Slaves:

Caroline, 36, and children, Jack, 9, Alfred, 7, and Haney, female, 6; Violet, 16, and Betsy, 11.

Book A-2, P 425 Succession of William S. McGough, January 1865, died 12 Nov 1864. Mentions widow, Elizabeth McGough, daughter, Frances Jane McGough, and son, Joseph R. McGough. Slaves: Eliza, 37, and children, Sarah, 7, Vicey, 5; John, 14, Setta, 10, Manuel, 16, and Nathan, 12.

Book A-3, P 346 Succession of Mary A. Wood, March 1865, died 7 Jul 1847. Mentions husband, Henry P. Anderson, daughters, Eliza Allice Anderson and Sarah Anderson, and son, William Henry Anderson. Slaves: Humphrey, 40, Dilley, 34, and her three chldren, not named.

Book A-2, P 192 Succession of Amy Ann Jones, April 1865, died 1864. Mentions husband, Joseph R. Parker. Slaves: Wesly, 16, and Jenny, 65.

Book A-3, P 157 Succession of Permelia Sloan, January 1865, died 1864. Mentions Delaware S. Jones, daughter of William O. Jones, deceased, and Permelia Sloan; Hugh Yongue, husband of Delaware S. Jones, Hiram A. Wilson, and James B. Wilson. Also mentions Loch Lomond Plantation. At a family meeting approved by the court, lots were drawn to establish ownership of slaves. Lot #1, Alfrey, 34, and children, William, 10, Lewis, 7, Napoleon, 8; George, 30, and Malissa, 57, drawn by Victoria A. Wilson. Lot #2, Martha, 27, and children, Lucinda, 10, Sarah, 8, Alice, 6, Desoto, 1, and John, 20 months, drawn by Hiram A. Wilson. Lot #3, Julia, 37, and son, Edmond, 5; Jim, 24, and Harvey, 12, drawn by James B. Wilson. Lot #4, Louisa, 25, and son, Benjamin, 4; Ellick, 50, and Becky, 11, drawn by Delaware S. Jones, wife of William O. Jones, deceased. Lot #5, Rassette, 16, Fidelia, 13, and Tom, 38, drawn by Delaware S. Jones (Yongue), daughter of Permelia Sloan.

Book E, P 506 Succession of William Brewster, April 1865, "departed this life at Vicksburg, Mississippi, on or about 5 Jul 1863." Mentions widow, Elizabeth Taylor, deceased, Hiram Brewster, administrator, minor sons, William W. Brewster and James M. Brewster, and minor daughter, Elizabeth Brewster. Slave: Bill, 24.

ABSTRACTS OF CONVEYANCES
(SLAVE DEEDS) 1839-1865

Book A, P 57
Know all men that I, Philip Feazel, in consideration of a negro woman named Lotte, formerly the property of John Donnelly, late of Dale County, Alabama, do hereby convey to John Donnelly a negro man called Oliver. (No ages shown.)

Deed not dated   Philip Feazel
                               John Donnelly
Witnesses: W. W. Farmer (his mark: X), John Taylor
Recorded 10 Aug 1840

Book A, P 57
Know ye all men that I, John Davis, for the sum of $800, have sold to John A. G. Davis, a negro woman named Caroline. (No age shown.)

18 Aug 1840   John Davis
                               John A. G. Davis
Witnesses: Wade H. Hough, J. B. Davis
Recorded 3 Nov 1840

Book A, P 58
Know ye all men that for the love I have for my beloved daughter, Elizabeth Odom, wife of John Odom, I grant unto her a negro woman, Margaret, 18.

15 Jul 1839   David Hendrick
                               Elizabeth Odom
Witnesses: John Boatright, James H. Black
Recorded 23 May 1840

Book A, P 62

Before me, John Taylor, Notary Public, came John Donnelly, who acknowledges that he sold to William W. Farmer a negro man named Joe, 30, for $800.

26 Aug 1840   John Donnelly
            William W. Farmer (his mark X)
Witnesses: Philip Feazel, Solomon Feazel
Recorded 26 Aug 1840

Book A, P 63
Before me, John Taylor, Parish Judge, appeared Robert Cook who declares he has sold to Daniel Payne a negro slave named Bob, 25, for $533.

7 Jan 1840   Robert Cook
            Daniel Payne
Witnesses: John H. Guice, Alvin W. McCormick
Recorded 7 Jan 1840

Book A, P 71
Before me, John Taylor, Parish Judge, appeared John H. Bryant, who declares that for $700, he has sold to John H. Lowery a negro slave named Sarah, 18.

31 Dec 1840   John H. Bryant
            John H. Lowery

Witnesses: W. C. Carr, W. C. Tate
Recorded 31 Dec 1840

Book A, P 72
Before me, John Taylor, Notary Public, came Willis Wood who states he has sold to Thomas T. Ratliff a slave girl named Patsey for $550. (No age shown.)

            Willis Wood
            Thomas T. Ratliff
Witnesses: Jock F. Lowery, Charles H. Raley
Recorded 5 Dec 1840

Book A, P 73

Before me, William C. Smith, Parish Recorder, came John Huey, who declares he sold to Mary Malery 2 negro slaves, Lucy, 17, and Jack, 14, for the sum of $800.

5 Dec 1840   John Huey
                             Mary Malery
Witnesses: John Auston (his mark: X), Richard Lee (his mark: X)
Recorded 5 Dec 1840

Book A, P 86
Before me, John Taylor, Parish Judge, appeared Maria Louisa Hendrick, now wife of John W. Pope, who declares she has sold to Lewis Chandler slaves, to wit, Betsy, 33, and child Caroline, 3, for $800.

18 Jan 1840   Maria Louisa Hendrick
                             Lewis Chandler
Witnesses: (names obscure)
Recorded 18 Jan 1841

Book A, P 94
Before me, John Taylor, Parish Judge, appeared Thomas J. Griffin, who acknowledges that in consideration of the sum of $700, he has sold to Henry P. Anderson, the slave girl, Audry, 30.

18 Oct 1841   Thomas J. Griffin
                             H. P. Anderson
Witnesses: David M. Harris, Charles H. Baley
Recorded 18 Oct 1841

Book A, P 95
Before me, John Taylor, Parish Judge, came John Faught and Susan Faught who declare they sold to James M. Turner 2 negro slaves, Lizzy, 39, and Mary, 13, for $2050.

4 Jul 1841   John Faught
                             James M. Turner
Witnesses: Charles N. Raley, William Bates (his mark: X)
Recorded 4 Jul 1841

Book A, P 97

Before me, John Taylor, Parish Judge, appeared W. W. Farmer, who declares he has sold to Philip Feazel a negro slave named Elijah, 55, for $820.
5 May 1841   W. W. Farmer (his mark: X)
                                             Philip Feazel
Witnesses: James Seale, William Sipes
Recorded 5 May 1841

Book A, P 98
Know ye all men that I, Robert Cook, of Ouachita Parish, have sold to Matthew Wood a slave named Bob, 24, for $1000.
30 Apr 1841   Robert Cook
                                             Matthew Wood
Witnesses: John Ray, H. J. Barker
Recorded 30 Apr 1841

Book A, P 110
Know ye all men that I, Noel Mixon, have sold to Permelia Ann Farmer two negro slaves, Elick, 35, and Mary 30, for $1700.
26 Jan 1841   Noel Mixon
                                             Permelia A. Farmer
Witnesses: James Huey 3d, John Rogers
Recorded 26 Jan 1841

Book A, P 114
In consideration of the love and affection I have for my son, Daniel Payne, I give to him for the sum of one dollar the slaves, Easter, 20, Moses, 7, and Charles, 3.
2 Dec 1840   Mary A. Payne (her mark: X)
                                             Daniel Payne
Witnesses: Thomas A. Wilson, Thomas Sawyer (his mark: X)
Recorded 16 Jan 1841

Book A, P 117
Know ye all men by these presents that I, William B. Easterling, have given to Spencer H. Easterling, son of Shadrack Easterling, the slave boy, Oliver. (No age or value shown.)
7 Jan 1840   William B. Easterling
                                             Spencer H. Easterling

Witness: Archibald McBride (Deed was executed in Simpson County, Mississippi, recorded in Union Parish 9 Oct 1840)

Book A, P 119
Know ye all men by these presents that I, John Donnelly, have swapped my slave, Olivia, for the slave of Philip Feazel, named Lott, a woman. (No ages shown.)
26 Aug 1840   John Donnelly
                                         Philip Feazel
Witnesses: W. W. Farmer, Solomon Feazel
Recorded 26 Aug 1840

Book A, P 134
Before me, Chichester Chaplian, Judge, Claiborne Parish, came Lawrence Scarborough who declares he has sold to Sarahe Scarborough a female slave named Molly, 50, for $300.
15 Oct 1839   Lawrence Scarborough
                                        Sarahe Scarborough
Witness: Chichester Chaplian, Judge (Deed was executed in Claiborne Parish, recorded in Union Parish 7 Dec 1841)

Book A, P 149
Before me, John Taylor, Parish Judge, appeared Philip Feazel, who states he has sold to W. W. Farmer 2 negro slaves, Elijah, 35, and his wife, Lott, 35, for $1500.
2 Nov 1841   Philip Feazel
                                       W. W. Farmer (his mark: X)
Witnesses: John Parker (his mark: X), Wm. Evans (his mark: X)
Recorded 2 Nov 1841

Book A, P 193
Be it known that in consideration of the love and affection I have for my daughter, Elvina Cooper, Wife of A. B. Cooper, I give to her for the sum of one dollar a female slave named Louisa, 11.
25 Nov 1839   James Seale
                                       Elvina Cooper
Witnesses: J. D. Cooper, A. J. Cooper (Deed was executed in Autauga County, Alabama, recorded in Union Parish 25 Nov 1839)

Book A, P 199
Before me, John Taylor, Parish Judge, appeared Lewis N. Shelton who declares he has sold to John Hill 2 female slaves, Charity, 19, and Penny, 17.

2 Mar 1844   Lewis N. Shelton
                         John Hill

Witness: John Taylor, Judge
Recorded 11 May 1844

Book A, P 270
Before me, John Taylor, Judge, personally appeared Elias Steen, a resident of Rankin County, Mississippi, who declares that for the sum of $450 he has sold to Henry P. Anderson, the negro slave, Rachel, 31.

11 Jan 1843   E. Steen
                         H. P. Anderson

Witnesses: Peter Pruitt, W. W. Watson
Recorded 11 Jan 1843

Book A, P 279
Before me, John Taylor, Parish Judge, appeared John H. Griffin, who declares he has sold to John A. Bayless 2 negro slaves, Easter, 30, and Nelson, 7, for $500.

22 Apr 1843   John H. Griffin
                       John A. Bayless

Witnesses: Alexander Taylor, John Taylor
Recorded 22 Apr 1843

Book A, P 286
Before me, B. E. Davis, Notary Public, appeared Don Pedro Acquilla Cook, who declares he has sold to Sherrard McCall Fenner, a resident of Ouachita Parish, 3 negro slaves: Charles, 26, his wife, Rosean, 18, and their daughter, Emily, for $1000.

1 Apr 1845   D. P. A. Cook
                       Sherrard McCall Fenner

Witnesses: Leroy Findley, B. E. Davis
Recorded 13 May 1845

Book A, P 287

Before me, John Taylor, Parish Judge, came William Degraffenried, who declares he has sold to Alex M. Taylor 2 slave boys, Jacob, 12 and Robert, 10, for $500.

30 Jan 1844   Wm. Degraffenried
                                 Alexander M. Taylor
Witnesses: John Matthews, James K. Taylor
Recorded 30 Jan 1844

Book A, P 297
Know ye all men that I, Thomas Wilhite, declare I am justly indebted to Hiram Azwell, a resident of Claiborne Parish, of the sum of $373, and I have mortgaged to him the negro slave, Jane, 14.

10 Jun 1844   Thomas J. Wilhite
                                 Hiram Azwell
Witnesses: John N. Farmer, Philemon Wilhite
Recorded 10 Jun 1844

Book A, P 300
Before me, Thomas Van Hook, Notary Public, came Humphrey Jemison, who declares he has sold to Manimus Deloney the following slaves and other property, to wit, Isaac, 23, Andrew, 40, Charlotte, 30, Malinda, 25, Jess, 23, and Mary, 35. Also a waggin (sic), 4 mules and a bay mare, all for the sum of $4000.

20 Nov 1845   Humphrey Jemison
                                 Manimus Deloney
Witnesses: Charles McLaughlin, William M. Lawrence
Recorded 20 Nov 1845

Book A, P 305
Before me, Thomas Van Hook, Notary Public, came Thomas Wilhite, who declares he sold to Ethelbert S. Franklin, a resident of the State of Arkansas, a negro girl named Jane, 15, for $450.

31 Jan 1843   Thomas J. Wilhite
                                 Ethelbert S. Franklin
Witnesses: William J. Payne, I. A. R. Van Hook
Recorded 31 Jan 1843

Book A, P 307

Before me, Thomas Van Hook, Notary Public, came Don Pedro Acquilla Cook who states that for $600 he has sold to James Ramsey a slave named Eliza, 24, and her children, Hoby, 4, and Ann, 2.

9 Oct 1843   D. P. A. Cook

James Ramsey (his mark: X)

Witnesses: John V. Robertson, Isaac A. R. Van Hook

Recorded 9 Oct 1843

Book A, P 321

Before me, John Taylor, Parish Judge, appeared James H. Willson and his wife Permilia Jones Willson, who declare they have brought into the parish of Union, from Willcox County, Alabama, 8 negroes, the property of Permilia Willson: Jim, 45, Charles, 25, Malice, 32, and children, George, 9, Martha, 7, Louisa, 5, James, 3, and John, 4 months old.

3 Jul 1843   John H. Willson

Permilia Willson

Witnesses: William Ham (his mark: X), William Roberts

Recorded 3 Jul 1843

Book A, P 328

Know ye all men by these presents that I, Joel Guice, have sold to Eliza Barton, for the sum of $500, with consent of her husband, C. T. Barton, negro slaves, to wit, Letty, 32, and her children, Novel, 4, and July Ann, 1.

19 Oct 1843   Joel Guice

Eliza Barton

Witnesses: Samuel Allen, Neely Fleming

Recorded 21 Oct 1843

Book A, P 332

Before me, John Taylor, Parish Judge, appeared David Hendrick, who declares he has sold to James E. Jones for $1400, 2 slaves, Sharper, 37, and Charles, 22.

6 Oct 1843   David Hendrick

James E. Jones

Witnesses: David Ward, C. H. Rakey

Recorded 6 Oct 1843

Book A, P 334
Before me, Benjamin E. Davis, Notary Public, appeared John J. Butler, who declares he has sold to Avery Breed a negro man, Philip, 29, for $550.

28 Oct 1843   John J. Butler
                               Avery Breed

Witnesses: Thomas Norsworthy, Robert C. Webb
Recorded 8 Nov 1843

Book A, P 339
Before me, John Taylor, Parish Judge, came Daniel Colvin who declares that, in consideration of a marriage contract about to take place between him and Catherine May, widow of the late William May, he has granted to said Catherine May 2 negro slaves, Alex, 25, and Sarah, 17.

1 Sep 1843   Daniel Colvin
                               Catherine May (her mark: X)

Witnesses: R. Nixon, James H. Seale
Recorded 1 Sep 1843

Book A, P 351
Know ye men that I, Angeline Thompson, have sold to Michael O'Neal a negro slave named Melissa, 40, for $350.

12 Dec 1843   Angeline Thompson
                               Michael O'Neal

Witnesses: John W. Farmer, George W. Brady
Recorded 23 Dec 1843

Book A, P 351
Know ye all men that we have sold to Michael O'Neal a slave named Melissa, 40, for $350.

23 Dec 1843   Mitty Ellin Hindes
                               M. L. Hindes
                               M. A. Hindes
                               A. D. Hindes
                               Angeline Thompson
                               Michael O'Neal

Witnesses: John N. Farmer, George W. Brady (his mark: X)
Recorded 23 Dec 1843

53

Book A, P 353
Received of Willis Wood the sum of $150 in payment for a slave girl, Matilda, 5.
22 Feb 1844   David E. Allen
                                        Willis Wood
Witnesses: James E. Lee, John Lewis
Recorded 22 Feb 1844

Book A, P 365
Before me, John Taylor, Parish Judge, appeared Nancy Allen who declares she has sold to Robert W. Richardson a negro girl, 13, named Rose, for $400.
25 Jan 1844   Nancy Allen (her mark: X)
                                        Robert W. Richardson
Witnesses: Hiram Cooper, Willis Wood
Recorded 25 Jan 1844

Book A, P 367
Before me, John Taylor, Parish Judge, appeared Samuel B. Farrar, who declares he has sold to Elijah W. Brown a negro woman, Martha, 17, for $500.
20 Feb 1844   Samuel B. Farrar
                                        Elijah W. Brown
Witnesses: William Roberts, Jourdan G. Taylor
Recorded 20 Feb 1844

Book A, P 368
Before me, Thomas Van Hook, Notary Public, came Cyrus B. Hendley and his wife, Nancy Hendley, who state they have sold to John Taylor a slave named Joe, 23, for $650.
20 Feb 1844   Cyrus B. Hendley
                                        John Taylor
Witnesses: Peter Pruitt, Miller Edwards
Recorded 20 Feb 1844

Book A, P 370
Know all men by these presents that I, David Hendrick, have sold to James E. Jones following slaves: Anderson, 30, Sarah, 37, and child

Miriah, 1, and Judah, 18, and her infant, Nicy, 3 months old, for $1638.

1 Feb 1844   David Hendrick
                                    James E. Jones
Witnesses: William J. Kelley, R. F. Rabun
Recorded 21 Feb 1844

Book A, P 374
Before me, John Taylor, Parish Judge, appeared Benjamin May who declares he has sold to Philip May a negro slave named Milley, 30, and her children, Peter, 6, Lewis, 3, and John, infant, for $800.

5 Mar 1844   Benjamin May
                                    Philip May
Witnesses: Thomas Van Hook, James Roan
Recorded 5 Mar 1844

Book A, P 375
Before me, John Taylor, Parish Judge, came Wiley Underwood, who states that for the sum of $400 he has sold to Samuel J. Larkin following slaves: Lucy, 20, and child, Luvenia, 6 months; Cargel, 30, his wife, Harriett, 17, and their child, 6 months old.

6 Mar 1844   Wiley Underwood
                                    Samuel J. Larkin
Witnesses: John Raley, Foster H. Dunkin
Recorded 6 Mar 1844

Book A, P 386
Before me, B. E. Davis, Notary Public, came Benjamin Sims who declares he sold to James Woosley certain slaves, Tom, 45, and his wife, 32; Emily, 11, Jerry, 9, Anthony, 6, and Lucinda, 2, for $2000.

9 Apr 1844   Benjamin Sims
                                    James Woosley
Witnesses: Lewis Lanier, Joel Kelley
Recorded 26 Apr 1844

Book A, P 388
Before me, B. E. Davis, Notary Public, appeared Benjamin Sims, who states he has sold to William F. Bond, for the sum of $700, 2 slaves, Charles, 40, and Salley, 35.

20 Apr 1844   Benjamin Sims
                                     William F. Bond
Witnesses: Joel Kelley, Malinda Davis (her mark: X)
Recorded 6 May 1844

Book A, P 392
Before me, John Taylor, Parish Judge, came Isaac R. Thacker, who
states he has sold to Willis Wood a slave woman Martha, 19, and her
child, Jane, 7 months, for $600.
7 May 1844   Isaac R. Thacker
                                     Willis Wood
Witnesses: James Roane, John Honeycutt
Recorded 7 May 1844

Book A, P 394
Before me, John Taylor, Notary Public, came Isaac R. Thacker of
Natchitoches Parish, who states he has sold to James Roane for
$1500, slaves, viz, Jack, 43, Solomon, 26, and Joe, 23.
7 May 1844   Isaac R. Thacker
                                     James Roane
Witness: B. Gibson
Recorded 7 May 1844

Book A, P 403
Know ye all men that I, William Raney, have sold to Reubin Drake a
negro slave named George, 40, for $900.
23 May 1844   William Raney
                                     Reubin Drake
Witnesses: Philip May, John Robertson
Recorded 15 Jul 1844

Book A, P 407
Before me, Benjamin E. Davis, Notary Public, appeared Moses W.
Bledsoe, who declares he has sold to V. I. Bird a slave named Phill (no
age shown), for $180.
6 Sep 1844   Moses W. Bledsoe
                                     V. I. Bird
Witnesses: William H. Vaneyham, W. W. Adams
Recorded 14 Sep 1844

Book A, P 415
Received of Berwell H. Jones $550, payment for slaves Penny, 32, and her child, Matilda, 10 months old.
16 Oct 1844   Nancy Allen (her mark: X)
                                   Berwell H. Jones
Witnesses: J. B. Dees, E. M. Aulds
Recorded 28 Oct 1844

Book A, P 438
Know all men that we, W. C. Carr and Sarah Carr, have sold to W. P. Theobalds a slave named Winney, and her child, Andy, for $750. (No ages shown.)
9 Aug 1844   W. C. Carr
                                  Sarah Carr
                                  W. P. Theobalds
Witnesses: John V. Robertson, James A. Seale
Recorded 30 Sep 1844

Book A, P 453
In consideration of the sum of $1100, I have sold to Robert W. Windes three slaves as named: Moses, 32, Mary, 18, and her son, Rolly, 4 months old.
6 May 1845   Samuel P. Windes
                                  Robert W. Windes
Witnesses: John Ray, John Hill
Recorded 6 May 1845

Book A, P 454
In consideration of the sum of $525, I have sold to O. H. P. Windes certain slaves, to wit, Martha, 17, and her son, John, 5 months.
6 May 1845   Saml Windes
                                  O. H. P. Windes
Witnesses: John Ray, John Hill
Recorded 6 May 1845

Book A, P 455
Received of Edward B. Windes the sum of $525, payment for 3 slaves, Jane, 20, and her children, Dorkis, 2, and Jasper, 1.

6 May 1845   Saml P. Windes
                                        Edward B. Windes
Witnesses: John Ray, John Hill
Recorded 6 May 1845

Book A-1, P 3
Before me, Thomas Van Hook, Notary Public, came Alexander
Walker, a resident of North Carolina, who states he has sold to
William J. Payne a slave girl named Mary, 18, for $556.
2 Mar 1846   Alexander Walker
                                        W. J. Payne
Witnesses: H. R. Bryant, D. B. Ramsey
Recorded 2 Mar 1846

Book A-1, P 7
Before me, Thomas Van Hook, Notary Public, came Samuel J. Larken
who states he has sold to Wiley Underwood a slave woman named
Tenor, 45, and a slave girl named Manery, 10, for $550.
9 Oct 1846   S. J. Larken
                                        Wiley Underwood
Witnesses: Avery Breed, M. McFarland
Recorded 9 Oct 1846

Book A-1, P 19
Be it known that in consideration of the love and affection I have for
my son, Leroy Findley, I give to him the following slaves, Amanda, 18,
and her children, William, 2, Winney, 3, and Milly, 7, for the sum of 1
dollar.
25 Sep 1846   Wm. C. H. Findley
                                        Leroy Findley
Witnesses: John M. Campbell, Samuel S. Kelly (Deed was executed in
Noshuba County, Mississippi, recorded in Union Parish 30 Oct 1846)

Book A-1, P 29
Know ye all men by these presents that I, Harriet Barr, have sold to S.
M. Barr of Catahoula Parish, for the sum of $660, a negro slave
named John, 22.
20 Oct 1846   Harriet Barr
                                        S. M. Barr

Witnesses: B. H. Jones, V. I. Bird
Recorded 25 Nov 1846

Book A-1, P 52
Before me, William C. Smith, Parish Recorder, appeared Elijah Groom, who declares he has sold to Needham M. Bryan, a man, 40, no name shown, for $325.

15 Jan 1847   Elijah Groom
                               Needham M. Bryan
Witnesses: H. B. Bryan, Henry B. Lassiter
Recorded 15 Jan 1847

Book A-1, P 54
Be it known that in consideration of the love and affection I have for my daughter, Zelphia Beaird, I have given in trust to my grandson, John W. Beaird, 4 negro slaves, Ginney, 23, and her children, Randal, 3, Liza, 2, and David, 1.

29 Mar 1847   Stephen Dunn
                               Zelphia Beaird (trustee)
Witness: David E. Davis, JP (Deed was executed in Bibb County, Alabama, recorded in Union Parish 4 Apr 1847).

Book A-1, P 67
Know ye all men that I have sold to Fielding Miller a negro woman named Patsey, 26, for $500.

26 Jan 1847   Thomas T. Ratliff
                               Fielding Miller
Witnesses: N. R. Bryan, Thomas Van Hook
Recorded 26 Jan 1847

Book A-1, P 82
Know ye all men by these presents that I, Thomas F. Ferrell, have sold to Jesse Brantley negro slaves, to wit, Jerry, 26, and Mary, his wife, 22, and their children, Patrick, 4, Emily, 3, and Peggy, 2, for $2200.

20 Feb 1847   Thomas F. Ferrell
                               Jesse Brantley
Witnesses: Stephen McGill, Hamilton Bailey
Recorded 20 Feb 1847

Book A-1, P 96
Before me, Clairborne M. Smith, Notary Public, appeared Peggy Poor who states she has sold to Mary Stewart a slave named Matilda, 2, for $145.50.

12 Sep 1846   Peggy Poor
                              Mary Louise Stewart, wife
                              of Thomas J. Stewart
Witnesses: Charles H. Raley, James Stroop
Recorded 12 Sep 1846

Book A-1, P 98
Received of Thomas J. Stewart the sum of $900, payment for a slave boy named Elexander, 21.

1 Mar 1847   Jeptha Hughs
                              Thomas J. Stewart
Witness: C. M. Smith
Recorded 20 Mar 1847

Book A-1, P 99
Received from John Traylor the sum of $325, payment for a negro girl, named Milla, 9.

14 Mar 1847   J. J. Daniel
                              John Traylor
Witnesses: John Hill, S. W. White
Recorded 19 Mar 1847

Book A-1, P 104
Because of the love and affection I have for her, I donate to Sarah Traylor a slave named Jina, 77, and her children, Emily, 7, Stephen, 6, Shelly, 4, and George, 2.

19 Mar 1847   Josiah C. Traylor
Witnesses: John Traylor, John Hill
Recorded 19 Mar 1847

Book A-1, P 115
Know all men that I have sold to James C. Manning a slave girl named Tena, 18, and her child, Martin, 2, for $675.

29 Mar 1847   George M. Savage
                              James C. Manning

Witnesses: G. W. Mays, D. M. Harris
Recorded 29 Mar 1847

Book A-1, P 123
Received of Alvin McCommac, $600 in payment for a slave boy
named Jerry, 25.
29 Mar 1847   James R. Guice
                                     Alvin W. McCommac
Witnesses: J. N. Raley, John Raley
Recorded 29 Mar 1847

Book A-1, P 133
By order of the 12th Judicial Court, I have transferred to Valinda
Thompson, the following slaves, in the case of Thomas versus
Thompson: Kitty, 20, and her children, John, 11, Eli, 9, Sarah, 7,
Elizabeth, 6, Jo, a boy, 3, and Jane, 1. (No value shown.)
7 Nov 1846   Avery Breed, Sheriff
                                     Sampson B. Thomas
                                     Valinda Thompson, grantee
Witness: C. M. Smith
Recorded 7 Nov 1846

Book A-1, P 139
Received of William Atkinson the sum of $775, payment for 2 slaves,
Tinah, 18, and her son, Martin, 2.
17 Jun 1847   James C. Manning
                                     William Atkinson
Witnesses: W. A. Darby, W. Underwood
Recorded 17 Jun 1847

Book A-1, P 140
Received of James C. Manning the sum of $540, payment for a female
slave named Sally, 17.
18 Jun 1847   Isaac C. Mays
                                     James C. Manning
Witnesses: W. A. Darby, M. McFarland
Recorded 18 Jun 1847

Book A-1, P 174

Know all men by these presents that I, Jesse Willson, have sold to H. P. Anderson two negro slaves, George Jenkins, 18, and John Harrison, 16, for $1613.

1 Feb 1847   Jesse Willson
           H. P. Anderson

Witnesses: John Taylor, W. W. C. Eubanks (Deed was executed in New Orleans, recorded in Union Parish 1 Feb 1847.)

Book A-1, P 182
Know ye all men that I have sold to Moses Pearson 2 slaves, Graves, 20, and Selph, a girl, 14, for $1000.

29 Nov 1847   Milton Pinkston
           Moses Pearson

Witnesses: D. M. Harris, J. E. Jones
Recorded 29 Nov 1847

Book A-1, P 184
Received of Elizabeth Williams the sum of $800, payment for a slave man named Adam, 40.

4 Oct 1847   Elijah Tabor
           Elizabeth Williams

Witness: G. W. Tubb
Recorded 4 Oct 1847

Book A-1, P 184
Received of Elizabeth Williams the sum of $800, payment for a slave woman (name obscure) and her children, Caroline, 4, Warren, an infant, and Martha, 2.

2 Nov 1847   R. F. Tubb
           Elizabeth Williams

Witness names not shown
Recorded 2 Nov 1847

Book A-1, P 186
Before me, William C. Smith, Parish Recorder, came John Taylor, who states he sold to Edward B. Windes a slave man named Joseph, 26, for $750.

6 Nov 1847   John Taylor
           Edward B. Windes

Witnesses: W. A. Darby, M. Johnson
Recorded 6 Nov 1847

Book A-1, P 206
Know ye all men that I have sold a slave boy named Caleb, 18, to
William Thompson, for $800.
14 Feb 1848   Manning H. Mann
                                  William Thompson
Witnesses: Reuben Ellis, H. Regenburg
Recorded 17 Jul 1848

Book A-1, P 211
Know all men that I have sold to Edward B. Windes a slave girl named
Ellen, 20, for $600.
10 Jan 1848   Ralph Jones
                                  Edward B. Windes
Witnesses: John W. Hendrick, Sara E. Hendrick
Recorded 19 Jan 1848

Book A-1, P 216
Before me, William C. Smith, Parish Recorder, came W. J. Payne, who
declares he has sold to Daniel Payne a negro slave named Mary, 20,
for $600.
2 Mar 1848   Wm. J. Payne
                                  Daniel Payne
Witnesses: B. B. West, Alex M. Taylor
Recorded 2 Mar 1848

Book A-1, P 218
Know ye all men by the natural love and affection I have for my
daughter, Harriett C. Dozier, wife of Dr. James A. Dozier, I, Harriett
C. Cann, have given to her 1 slave named Betty, 6.
15 Nov 1846   Harriett C. Cann
                                  Harriett R. Dozier
Witnesses: B. R. Jeffries, George N. Ware (Deed was executed in
Perry County, Alabama, recorded in Union Parish 19 Nov 1846.)

Book A-1, P 220

Know ye all men by these presents that I, Aaron Van Hook, have sold to David B. Briggs a negro girl named Caroline, 17, for $562.50.

15 Mar 1848   Aaron Van Hook
                                      David B. Briggs
Witnesses: Wiley Underwood, W. H. Parkey
Recorded 15 Mar 1848

Book A-1, P 222
Know all men that I have sold to William Thompson a slave named Martha, 25, for $600.

14 Mar 1848   Aaron Van Hook
                                      William Thompson
Witnesses: Reuben Ellis, W. G. Kelley
Recorded 14 Mar 1848

Book A-1, P 225
Received of John Smith, $800, payment for James, a slave boy, 17.

17 Mar 1848   I. T. Henderson
                                      John Smith
Witness: Reuben Ellis
Recorded 17 Mar 1848

Book A-1, P 230
Know ye all men by these presents that I, Hugh Hagen, have sold to Royal K. Love a negro slave named Duncan M. Cowan, 21, for the sum of $800.

14 Mar 1848   Hugh Hagen
                                      Royal K. Love
Witnesses: Wm. B. Hall, John G. Hill (Deed was executed in New Orleans, Louisiana, recorded in Union Parish 3 Apr 1848.)

Book A-1, P 234
Before me, William C. Smith, Parish Recorder, came Randolph and Elizabeth Hester, to declare they sold to Thomas J. Wilhite a slave woman named Getta and her child, Alexander, 5, for the sum of $800.

10 Aug 1848   Randolph Hester
                                      Thomas J. Wilhite
Witnesses: W. Underwood, W. A. Darby
Recorded 15 Aug 1848

Book A-1, P 243
Be it remembered that before me, William C. Smith, Parish Recorder, appeared Philip May who declares he has sold to Powhatten Boatright a negro slave named Patsey, between 20 and 25, for $500.

27 Dec 1847   Philip May
                            Powhatten Boatright

Witnesses: Moses Pearson, J. V. Butler
Recorded 27 Dec 1847

Book C, P 5
Before me, W. C. Smith, Parish Recorder, appeared Mary Mathews, wife of Comer B. Mason, to declare she has sold to Campbell Lassiter negro slaves, to wit, Judy, 33, and children, Ephrem, 4, and Hetty, 2, for $1500.

29 Jul 1848   Mary A. Mathews
                            C. B. Mason

Witnesses: H. Regenburg, Uriah Westbrooks
Recorded 29 Jul 1848

Book C, P 15
Before me, William C. Smith, Parish Recorder, appeared Aaron Van Hook, who states that he has sold to Berwell H. Jones, for $4850, following slaves, on behalf of minors, Louisa Jones and Richard Jones, Berwell H. Jones being the natural tutor: Aaron, 20, Jane, 17, Gabriel, 22, Matthew, 22, and Handy, 24.

15 Nov 1848   Aaron Van Hook
                            Berwell H. Jones, natural tutor

Witnesses: P. May, H. Regenburg
Recorded 15 Nov 1848

Book C, P 16
Know all men that I have sold to John L. Willson for the sum of $988, certain slaves, Joe, 45, Caroline, 23, and her children, John, 6, and Prince, 5

12 May 1848   James J. Steadley
                            John L. Willson

Witnesses: V. I. Bird, J. H. Willson
Recorded 21 May 1848

Book C, P 39
Be it known that we have sold to Campbell Lassiter for the sum of $500, a negro woman named Mary, 30.

22 Jan 1849   Mary A. Mathews
                                              C. B. Mason
Witnesses: James E. Lee, W. M. Lawrence
Recorded 22 Jan 1849

Book C, P 49
In consideration of the love and affection I have for my daughter, Florida C. Bryan, wife of Lucien Bryan, I, James Pace, grant unto her a slave girl named Harriett, 12.

6 Dec 1848   James Pace
                                              Florida C. Bryan
Witnesses: Henry R. Bryan, N. M. Bryan
Recorded 12 Apr 1849

Book C, P 49
Know all men by these presents that I, John W. Hendrick, in consideration of the sum of $879, have sold to James E. Jones, the following negro slaves: Jim, 41, Mariah and children, Martha, 8, Mary, 6, Henry, 5, Sam, 2, and John, 16 months old.

7 Feb 1849   John W. Hendrick
                                              James E. Jones
Witnesses: Eli L. Collins, D. R. Delk
Recorded 7 Feb 1849

Book C, P 68
This contract of sale entered into between party of first part, Henry B. Lassiter, and party of second part, H. R. Bryan, party of first part selling to party of second part certain slaves, viz, Polly, 30, and her child, Ann, 9; Sarah, 15, and infant, John, 10 months, for the total sum of $650.

18 Mar 1848   Henry B. Lassiter
                                              H. R. Bryan
Witnesses: H. Regenburg, Jacob Gibson
Recorded 15 May 1848

Book C, P 76
Before me, Claiborne Smith, Notary Public, came Aaron Van Hook, who declares he has sold to Malinda Davis a slave named Malinda, 17, for the sum of $567.50.
13 Mar 1848   Aaron Van Hook
                                     Malinda Davis (her mark: X)
Witnesses: W. A. Darby, W. Underwood
Recorded 13 Mar 1848

Book C, P 82
Know ye all men that I, George W. Honeycutt, have sold to Philip Feazel for $550, a slave named Sarah, 14.
11 Dec 1848   George W. Honeycutt
                                     Philip Feazel
Witnesses: H. Regenburg, Ephriam Hopkins
Recorded 11 Dec 1848

Book C, P 89
Know all men that I, Martin Mims, have sold to James C. Manning a negro slave girl named Phebe, 18, for $655.
24 Mar 1849   Martin Mims
                                     James C. Manning
Witnesses: (names obscure)
Recorded 24 Mar 1849

Book C, P 98
Know ye all men that we, Elizabeth Dees and J. B. Dees, have sold to Martin Hendrick a slave girl named Zima, 18, for $700.
8 Feb 1848   Elizabeth Dees
                                     J. B. Dees
                                     Martin Hendrick
Witnesses: Richard Dean, M. Armstrong
Recorded 4 Apr 1848

Book C, P 100
Know ye all men by these presents that I, George Haywood, of Union County, Arkansas, have sold to Robert Webb, a resident of Union Parish, for $2300, the following negro slaves, to wit, Edmond, 23, Dick, 23, and Charles, 21.

4 Jul 1848   George W. Haywood
                           Robert C. Webb

Witnesses: (names obscure)
Recorded 4 Jul 1848

Book C, P 109
In consideration of the sum of $550, we have sold a slave girl named Pheby, 18, to Martin Mims.
23 Feb 1849   Caroline L. Wise
                           Mary Foster
                           George Lambright
                           Adeline Smith
                           Martin Mims

Witness: William Pipes
Recorded 23 Feb 1849

Book C, P 108
Know ye all men that I, J. E. Tomlinson, have sold a negro boy named Jesse, 10, to James Pettitt for $300.
3 Apr 1849   John E. Tomlinson
                           James Pettitt

Witnesses: Thomas D. Jones, C. L. Norman
Recorded 3 Apr 1849

Book C, P 112
Received of N. M. Bryan the sum of $800, in payment for a slave named Wiley, 21.
6 Mar 1849   W. O. Jones
                           N. M. Bryan

Witnesses: H. B. Lassiter, W. R. Bryan
Recorded 15 Apr 1849

Book C, P 113
In consideration of the sum of $700, I have sold to William O Jones following slaves: Betty, 24, and children, Phill, 2, and (girl, 5, name obscure), and a negro man, Wiley, 22.
5 Apr 1849   Needham M. Bryan
                           William O. Jones

Witnesses: H. R. Bryan, Henry Lassiter

Recorded 13 Apr 1849

Book C, P 138
Be it remembered that I, Campbell Lassiter, for the sum of $550, have sold to Mary Jarman a negro woman named May, about 30.
14 May 1849   Campbell Lassiter
                               Mary Jarman
Witnesses: G. A. Hammond, Thos Van Hook
Recorded 14 May 1849

Book C, P 145
Received of Robert McGough the sum of $575, payment for a negro slave girl named Jane, 17.
27 Feb 1849   Aaron Van Hook
                               Robert McGough
Witnesses: Alex M. Taylor, C. M. Smith
Recorded 27 Feb 1849

Book C, P 146
Know all men that I have sold to James M. Traylor a slave boy named Bud, 17, for $755.
15 Jun 1849   George Rephart
                               James M. Traylor
Witness: H. B. Dawson
Recorded 15 Jun 1849

Book C, P 149
Know ye that I, George W. Rephart, have sold to James M. Traylor a slave boy named Buck, 17, for $775.
13 Jun 1849   George W. Rephart
                               J. M. Traylor
Witnesses: H. B. Essick, Josiah C. Traylor
Recorded 13 Jun 1849

Book C, P 160
This contract of sale made between William O. Jones, to sell to N. M. Bryan negro slaves, Betty, and her child, Lizzy, for the sum of $1300. (No ages shown.)
6 Jun 1849   W. O. Jones

N. M. Bryan
Witnesses: W. R. Bryan, Brice Jones
Recorded 30 Jun 1849

Book C, P 170
Be it remembered that in consideration of the love and affection I have for my daughter, Mary Dick, formerly Mary Meadows, I, Rawson Meadows, give to her 2 slaves, Martha, 10, and Peggy, 30 to 40 years old, for the sum of one dollar in hand.
1 May 1849   Rawson Meadows
Witnesses: John Pratt, Whitfield Lindsay (Deed was executed in Tallapoosa County, Alabama, recorded in Union Parish 1 May 1849)

Book C, P 172
Know ye all men by these presents that I, Joseph F. Roberts of the State of Mississippi and County of Kemper, in consideration of the sum of $4895, have sold to Martha M. Andrews, negro slaves: Joe, 50, Shedrick, 30, Elijah, 15, Charly, 13, Julia, 11, Caroline, 9, Winston, 7, Stephen, 5, Mary, 3, Betsy, 20, and child, and Beck, 36, and child. (No name or age shown.)
5 Sep 1849   Joseph F. Roberts
                                               Martha M. Andrews
Witnesses: B. F. Dillard, George A. Hammond
Recorded 5 Sep 1849

Book C, P 173
Know ye all men by these presents that I, Joseph F. Roberts of Mississippi, County of Kemper, for the sum of $1575, have sold to John R. Andrews, 5 negro slaves, viz, Isaac, 35, Charity, 55, Julia, 25, and her two children. (No names or ages shown.)
5 Sep 1849   Joseph F. Roberts
                                               John R. Andrews
Witnesses: B. G. Dillard, George A. Hammond
Recorded 5 Sep 1849

Book C, P 177
I, Eliza Foy, now wife of Berwell Jones, donate to my children, Louisa Jones and Richard Jones, because of love and affection entertained for them, certain slaves, to wit, Abrom, 30, value $700. A

70

negro woman, Handy, 25, value $800. A woman, Cory, 20, value $600. A woman, Dofney, 29, value $400, and her child, Phebia, 6 months, value $150. A man, Swaney, 18, $700. Little Rose, 28, value $500. Lucinda, 30, value $350. Matilda, 10, value $250. Frances, 15, value $400. Allen, 10, value $300. Jim, 8, value $300. Peter, 2, value $200. Nelson, 4 months, value $100. Big Ann, 18, value $600. Big Martin, 20, value $600. Mary Ann, 14, value $400. Little Martin, 11, value $400.

3 Oct 1849   Eliza Foy
Witnesses: A. Armstrong, V. I. Bird
Recorded 3 Oct 1849

Book C, P 185
Know ye all men that we, Mary J. Colvin and C. H. Colvin have sold to N. M. Bryan 3 negro slaves, Betsy, 22, and her children, Lizzy, 5, and Phill, 15 months, for $700.

3 Feb 1849   Mary J. Colvin
                              C. H. Colvin
                              N. M. Bryan
Witness: A. Middleton (Deed was executed in Lowndes County, Alabama, recorded in Union Parish 8 Nov 1849)

Book C, P 202
Know ye all men that I, William T. H. Manning, have sold to John Odom a slave named Henrietta, 10, for $420.

3 Apr 1849   W. T. H. Manning
                              John Odom
Witnesses: John W. Hendrick, Martin Hendrick
Recorded 28 Nov 1849

Book C, P 216
Know ye all men that I, Mary Roberts, for the sum of $1600 and one wagon, have sold to Robert H. Andrews, 5 negro slaves, viz, Sarah, 65, Mariah, 36, Nancy, 11, Emily, 8, and Eliza, 6.

5 Jan 1850   Mary P. Roberts
                              Robert H. Andrews
Witnesses: T. M. Heard, Robert Sapiter
Recorded 5 Jan 1850

Book C, P 218
Before me, William C. Smith, Parish Recorder, came Elizabeth Hendrix, wife of Hiram Hendrix, who states she has sold certain slaves, to Thomas T. Ratliff for $1053.40, viz, George, 33, Anney, 24, and her child, Georgy Ann, 3.

8 Jan 1850   Elizabeth Hendrix
         Thomas T. Ratliff
Witnesses: James H. Carson, R. Delk
Recorded 8 Jan 1850

Book C, P 219
Know ye all men that I, Webb Kidd, have sold a negro woman named Mary, 22, to Webb Kidd Junior, for $625.

24 Aug 1849   Webb Kidd
         Webb Kidd Jr
Witnesses: N. A. Kidd, Albert A. Kidd
Recorded 25 Aug 1849

Book C, P 230
Know all men that I have sold to George W. Reynolds for $2200, 2 slaves, Isom, a boy, 23, and Martha, 21.

22 Oct 1849   Wm. H. Crawford
         G. W. Reynolds
Witness: John N. Farmer
Recorded 4 Dec 1849

Book C, P 253
Know all men that I have sold to Benjamin B. West a slave named Daniel, 30, for the sum of $940.

12 Dec 1849   Albert Honeycutt
         Benjamin B. West
Witnesses: Thomas Van Hook, W. A. Darby
Recorded 19 Dec 1849

Book C, P 255
Know all men that I have sold to James H. Willson a slave named Nicy and her child, Caroline, 10, for $1000.

22 Jun 1849   William O. Jones
         J. H. Willson

Witnesses: David Payne, B. F. Dillard
Recorded 22 Jun 1849

Book C, P 260
Before me, Claiborne M. Smith, Notary Public, came William T. H.
Manning who declares he sold to Robert W. Windes a slave named
Cheny, 45, and her children, Jerry, 2, and Joe, 3, for $700.
4 Jun 1849   Wm. T. H. Manning
                                       R. W. Windes
Witness: George A. Hammond
Recorded 4 Jun 1849

Book C, P 316
Know ye all men that I, George Davis, have sold to Evaline Riordan 3
negro slaves, Addison, 35, Bill, 25, and Don, 20, for the sum of $500.
25 Mar 1844   George Davis
                                       Evaline Riordan
Witness: Wm. C. Smith, Recorder
Recorded 18 Jan 1847

Book C, P 325
Before me, B. E. Davis, Notary Public, came John C. Shores, who
states that for $575 he has sold to Ann Underwood a girl named
Perliney, 18, and her child, Ellen, 8 months.
14 Nov 1844   John C. Shores
                                       Ann Underwood
Witnesses: G. W. Sims, William G. Glasson (his mark: X)
Recorded 14 Nov 1844

Book C, P 328
Before me, Benjamin E. Davis, Notary Public, appeared Donald
McDonald, who states he has sold to William F. Bond two negro
slaves, Charles, 40, and Sally, 35, for $700.
20 Apr 1844   Donald McDonald
                                       Wm. F. Bond
Witnesses: Malinda D. Davis, Joel Kelley
Recorded 20 Apr 1844

Book C, P 333

Received of Sherard McFenner the sum of $1000, payment for three slaves, Charles, 26, his wife Rosean, 18, and their child Emily, 1.

13 May 1843   Don P. A. Cook
                                     Sherard McFenner

Witnesses: Leroy H. Findley, Lewis Lancer
Recorded 13 May 1843

Book D, P 3
Be it remembered that we, Cassandra Smith and Luke Smith, her husband, have sold to Henry Gersen a negro girl named Caroline, 14, for $400.

10 Feb 1845   Cassandra Smith
                                     Luke H. Smith
                                     Henry Gersen

Witnesses: John V. Robertson, John Atwell
Recorded 24 Feb 1845

Book D, P 7
Before me, B. E. Davis, Notary Public, came William Thompson who declares that for $700 he has sold to John Odom a slave named George, 25.

27 Feb 1845   William Thompson
                                     John Odom

Witnesses: Uriah M. Darden, John Norsworthy
Recorded 27 Feb 1845

Book D, P 13
Know ye all men that I, Daniel Payne, have sold to Henry Gersen a negro man named George, 22, for $600.

24 Mar 1845   Daniel Payne
                                     Henry Gersen

Witnesses: Thomas Van Hook, William M. Lawrence
Recorded 9 Apr 1845

Book D, P 14
Know ye all men that I, John McCaskey, of Montgomery County, Alabama, have paid to Jake Dillard, executor of the estate of William Wilson, $350 for a negro girl named Lucy (no age shown), for the

benefit of Elizabeth Hendrick, daughter of said William Wilson, deceased.

14 Jan 1845   John McCaskey
                                   Jake Dillard

Witness: W. A. Watson (Deed was executed in Montgomery County, Alabama, recorded in Union Parish 14 Jan 1845)

Book D, P 15
Know ye all men that I have sold to Josiah C. Traylor a slave girl, Charlotte, 16, for $700.

26 Feb 1845   James A. McHatton
                                   Josiah C. Traylor

Witnesses: John Hill, Henry Frillson
Recorded 6 May 1845

Book D, P 17
Know ye all men by these presents that I, George M. Savage, have sold to George H. Knox for $600, a negro man named Jerry, 31.

23 May 1845   George M. Savage
                                   George H. Knox

Witnesses: H. R. Bryan, B. F. Dillard
Recorded 23 May 1845

Book D, P 18
Know all men by these presents that I have sold to George M. Savage, for the sum of $650, a slave man named Jerry, 31.

23 May 1845   William J. Payne
                                   George M. Savage

Witnesses: B. F. Dillard, A. R. Bryan
Recorded 23 May 1845

Book D, P 19
In consideration of the sum of $575, I have sold to Oliver H. P. Windes, a slave named Hamilton, 18.

24 Mar 1845   James A. McHatton

Witnesses: John Hill, R. C. Martin
Recorded 24 Mar 1845

Book D, P 20

I, Daniel Payne, acknowledge that I have sold to Henry Gersen negro slaves, to wit, Easther, 25, and her son Charles, 7, for $700.
24 May 1845   Daniel Payne
                                     Henry Gersen
Witnesses: Fielding Miller, D. H. Quilling
Recorded 24 May 1845

Book D, P 21
I, Berry Fuller, a resident of Union Parish, declare that I have sold to Henry Gersen a negro girl, Edy, about 18 years old, for $425.
23 May 1845   B. Fuller
                                     Henry Gersen
Witnesses: Thomas Van Hook, William M. Lawrence
Recorded 23 May 1845

Book D, P 32
Know ye all men that I, John H. Griffin, in consideration of the love and affection I have for my niece, Martha Ann Griffin, wife of Simpson W. Ramsey, have given to her, for the sum of one dollar, negro slaves, to wit, Malina, 17, and her children, Martin, 5, Epsa, 2, and Joseph, 10 months. I also give to Martha Ann Griffin, Jane, a girl, 14.
8 Aug 1845   John H. Griffin
                                     Martha Ann Ramsey
Witnesses: Matthew R. More, Thomas L. Moore
Recorded 23 Sep 1845

Book D, P 33
In consideration of the affection I have for my son, Josiah Traylor, I give to him the following slaves, Vina, 25, and her children, Emily, 5, Stephen, 4, Shelby, 2, and an infant, 4 days old.
1 Sep 1845   Sarah Traylor (her mark: X)
Witnesses: John Traylor, Thomas M. Smith
Recorded 1 Sep 1845

Book D, P 49
Know ye all men that we, L. T. Kolb and James G. Kolb, have sold to Mary Green the slaves Kesiah, and her children, Elviny and Dilcy, for $950. (No ages shown.)
2 Oct 1845   L. T. Kolb

James G. Kolb
Mary Green

Witnesses: John Smith, John Feazel
Recorded 2 Oct 1845
Book D, P 70
Know all men that I have sold to James M. Turner a man named Jeff, 31, a boy, Foster, and a girl, Sarah, for $1400.
5 Dec 1845   Henry C. Turner
                            James M. Turner
Witnesses: Henry R. Bryan, Fielding Miller
Recorded 26 Jan 1846

Book D, P 90
Know ye all men that I, Milton Pinkston, of Bibb County, Alabama, have sold to James E. Jones a negro girl named Sally, 15, for $425.
11 Feb 1846   Milton Pinkston
                            James E. Jones
Witnesses: John W. Hendrick, Sarah A. Hendrick
Recorded 17 Feb 1846

Book D, P 94
Know all men that I, Joseph D. Christian, have sold to James H. Willson Slaves as named, for sums indicated: Jefferson, 27, for $400. Madison, 13, for $500. William, 4, for $150. Gabriel, 7, for $200. Jane, 11, for $300. Jourdan, 2, for $150.
5 Feb 1846   J. D. Christian
                            J. H. Willson
Witnesses: H. R. Bryan, N. M. Bryan
Recorded 2 Mar 1846

Book D, P 98
Know ye all men that I, Sarah Grammont Cabreard, have sold to Lucian Larch a slave boy, Alfred, 35, for $280.
12 Jul 1845   Sarah Grammont Cabreard
                            (her mark: X)
                            L. Larch
Witnesses: Lewis Autrey, Henry Hobbs
Recorded 23 Mar 1846

Book D, P 105
Before me, William C. Smith, Notary Public, came John A. G. Davis who declares he has sold to James Roane a slave named Caroline and her child (No name or age shown; no value shown.) Slaves were acquired by Davis from John D. Jarman and Matilda Jarman.

13 Apr 1846   J. A. G. Davis
                        James Roane
Witnesses: N. M. Bryan, D. K. Quilling
Recorded 14 Apr 1846

Book D, P 106
Know all men that I have sold to Edward B. Windes, a slave woman, Mariah, 23, for $500.

5 May 1846   H. C. Bartlet
                        E. B. Windes
Witnesses: John Edwards, James M. Nall
Recorded 5 May 1846

Book D, P 107
Received of Eli Owen $300 in payment for a female slave named Bicea, 10.

21 May 1846   H. Funderburk
                        Eli Owen
Witnesses: A. B. George, H. C. Glasson
Recorded 21 May 1846

Book D, P 110
Received of J. C. Traylor, $600, in payment for Joanna, 17, and her daughter, Caroline, 6 months, both negro slaves.

17 Feb 1846   Sherman Johnson
                        J. C. Traylor
Witnesses: William Evell, John Hill
Recorded 25 May 1846

Book D, P 112
Know ye that I have sold to P. B. Traylor of Union Parish 2 negro slaves, Frances, 12, and Joe, 12, for $750.

15 Mar 1846   Mark Davis

Witnesses: James A. Powell, Henry Frillson (Deed was executed in New Orleans, recorded in Union Parish 25 May 1846)

Book D, P 114
Received of James M. Traylor, $650, payment for Mary, 23, and her son, Joe, 5, both slaves
21 Mar 1846   Samuel Traylor
                                           James M. Traylor
Witnesses: John Hill, Thomas Bradford
Recorded 25 May 1846

Book D, P 115
Know ye all men that I, M. Davis, for the sum of $750, have sold to P. B. Traylor, Joe, 12, and Francis, 14, negro slaves.
5 Mar 1846   Mark Davis
                                          P. B. Traylor
Witnesses: James M. Powell, Henry Frillson
Recorded 25 May 1846

Book D, P 121
We, Mileet Love and Royal K. Love, acknowledge we have sold to David Hendrick a slave woman, Harriett, 28, and her child, Mira, 2 months old, for $550.
22 Dec 1845   Mileet Love (her mark: X)
                                          David Hendrick
Witnesses: B. E. Davis, James Robinson
Recorded 22 Dec 1845

Book D, P 121
Know ye all men that I, Mileet Love, have sold to David Hendrick, tutor of Harriett E. Manning, minor heir of Roland Manning, deceased, a female slave named Sharlot, 28, and her child, Mira, 2 months old, for $550.
22 Dec 1845   Mileet Love (her mark: X)
                                          David Hendrick, tutor
Witnesses: Jared Robinson, B. E. Ellis
Recorded 17 Jun 1846

Book D, P 125

Know ye all men that in consideration of the sum of $500 I, Pinckney
Odom, have sold to E. M. Aulds, a negro slave named Lucy, 30.
1 Mar 1850   Pinckney Odom
                                              E. M. Aulds
Witnesses: W. A. Darby, W. C. Carr
Recorded 11 Mar 1850

Book D, P 162
Before me, Reuben Ellis, Parish Recorder, came Solomon Powell who
declares he has given to his wife, Elizabeth Ann Green, slaves named
Gabriel, 24, and Mary, 28.
3 May 1850   Solomon Powell
                                              Ann Powell
Witnesses: Abraham Levison, J. B. Wallace
Recorded 3 May 1850

Book D, P 169
Before me, Reuben Ellis, Notary Public, came N. M. Bryan, who
states he has sold a negro girl named Charity (no age shown) for $600,
to William Thompson.
27 Apr 1850   N. M. Bryan
Witnesses: H. R. Bryan, J. T. Henderson
Recorded 27 Apr 1850

Book D, P 173
Know all ye men that I, Needham M. Bryan, for the sum of $630, have
sold to Reuben Ellis a negro slave girl named Emely, 19.
27 Apr 1850   Needham M. Bryan
                                              Reuben Ellis
Witnesses: S. T. Henderson, H. R. Bryan
Recorded 27 Apr 1850

Book D, P 178
Know ye all men that I have sold to John Steel, for $675, Gracey, 32,
and her son, Caswell, 14 months.
26 Mar 1850   Samuel B. Steel
                                              John Steel
Witnesses: A. H. Courtney
Recorded 13 Jun 1850

Book D, P 185
Before me, Reuben Ellis, Parish Recorder, appeared Arrena
Thompson, administrator of the estate of W. B. Thompson, deceased,
who states she has sold to James K. Love slaves of the estate, for
$800: Milly, 35, and children, Caroline, 3, Tennessee, 8 months, and a
negro girl named Charity, 18.
14 Jun 1850   Arrena Thompson
                                     James K. Love
Witnesses: Henry Phelps, Josiah Holt
Recorded 14 Jun 1850

Book D, P 186
Before me, Reuben Ellis, Notary Public, came James K. Love who
states he has sold to Anna Thompson a slave girl named Charity, 18,
for $300.
14 Jun 1850   James K. Love
Witnesses: Henry Phelps, Josiah Holt
Recorded 15 Jun 1850

Book D, P 187
Know ye all men by these presents that I, Martin Mims, have sold to
B. F. Dillard the negro boy named Phil, about 10 years old, for $500.
21 Jun 1855   Martin Mims
                                     B. F. Dillard
Witnesses: Henry Regenburg, E. Whitson
Recorded 21 Jun 1855

Book D, P 196
Know all men that I have sold a slave man, Isha, 23, to Liberty K.
Thomas, for $1000.
4 Apr 1850   Martin Mims
Witnesses: Henry Regenburg, James B. Glasson
Recorded 15 Jun 1850

Book D, P 198
Before me, Reuben Ellis, Notary Public, came S. M. Farmer who
states that he has sold a slave man, Edd, 13, to Benjamin M. Tubb, for
$575.

21 Aug 1850   Shepard Farmer
                                     Benjamin M. Tubb
Witnesses: C. T. Barton, R. Tubb
Recorded 21 Aug 1850

Book D, P 216
Know ye all men that I, George W. Squires, have sold to Samuel J. Larkin for $850, a negro man named Jackson, 20.
21 May 1850   George W. Squires
                                     Samuel J. Larkin
Witnesses: Charles W. Phillips, Frank Williams
Recorded 5 Aug 1850

Book D, P 242
Received of Joshua Seale $100 in payment for a female slave named Fillis, 9 months old.
3 Apr 1850   Joseph Brent Seale
                                     Joshua Seale
Witness: Josiah Parker
Recorded 12 Oct 1850

Book D, P 242
Received of Lewis P. Seale the sum of $600 for a female named Hagar, 20.
12 Oct 1850   Joshua Seale
                                     Lewis P. Seale
Witness: Reuben Ellis, Notary
Recorded 12 Oct 1850

Book D, P 250
Know ye all men that I, Thomas Hinton, have sold to Obadiah Smith a negro slave named Sarah (no age shown) for $475.
29 Dec 1845   Thomas Hinton
                                     Obadiah Smith
Witnesses: B. F. Ford, John P. Smith
Recorded 29 Oct 1850

Book D, P 254

Be it known that in consideration of the love and affection I have for Mary Ann B. Manning, wife of W. T. Manning, I have given to her 2 slaves, namely, Harry, 15, and Major, 9.

26 Sep 1850
B. B. West
Mary Ann B. Manning

Witnesses: David Rabun, Pinckney Mann (his mark: X)
Recorded 26 Sep 1850

Book D, P 279
Before me, Reuben Ellis, Parish Recorder, appeared James H. Sewel who declares he sold to Harrison Pool a female slave, about 17 years, named Fanny, for $450.

19 Nov 1850
James H. Sewel
Harrison Pool (his mark: X)

Witnesses: John H. Masterson, Lewis Graves
Recorded 19 Nov 1850

Book D, P 293
Know all whom it may concern that for the love and affection we have for our beloved daughter Sarah Ann Abbott, we, Luke Smith and Cassandra Smith have given to her the negro girl, Bets, aged 10 or 11 (value not shown).

18 Dec 1850
Luke Smith
Cassandra Smith
Sarah Ann Abbott

Witnesses: N. M. Bryan, W. O. Jones
Recorded 18 Dec 1850

Book D, P 300
This contract of sale made between Banks A. Smith and Samuel A. Smith, party of the first part selling to party of second part, 2 slaves, to wit, a negro woman named Prissilla, 28, and Jim, 55, for $1950.

23 Dec 1850
Banks A. Smith
Samuel A. Smith

Witnesses: W. R. Bryan, James King
Recorded 23 Dec 1850

Book D, P 303

Know all men that I have sold to J. E. Jones 4 negro slaves, Elizabeth, 30, Solomon, 10, Jane, 7, and Nancy, 5, for $1487.
1 May 1850   Aaron Van Hook
                                           James E. Jones
Witnesses: W. A. Darby, W. M. Lawrence
Recorded 4 Jan 1851

Book D, P 323
Know ye all men by these presents that I, Martha M. Andrews, have sold to H. K. Dobey, a negro girl named Caroline, for $425.
15 Jan 1851   Martha M. Andrews
                                           H. K. Dobey
Witnesses: R. H. Andrews, John T. Roberts
Recorded 16 Jan 1851

Book D, P 331
Know ye all men that I, James A. Telford, of the county of Carroll, in Mississippi, in consideration of the sum of $700, have sold to Alfred Ford negro slaves, viz. Eliza, 22, Jack, 10, and Mary, 1.
1 Jan 1851   James A. Telford
                                           Alfred Ford
Witnesses: B. B. West, G. R. Carroll (Deed was executed in Carroll County, Mississippi, recorded in Union Parish 18 Feb 1851)

Book D, P 340
Before me, Reuben Ellis, Notary Public, came Josiah T. Williams, who swears he has sold to Jesse Odom, Maria, 32, and her child, Delia, 5 weeks, for $650.
4 Jan 1851   J. T. Williams
                                           Jesse Odom
Witnesses: Hiram D. Goyne (his mark: X), C. T. Barton
Recorded 4 Jan 1851

Book D, P 352
Be it known that for the sum of $600, I have sold to Lemuel Denson a negro slave, Polly, about 14 years old.
18 Mar 1851   Isaac Denson
                                           Lemuel Denson
Witnesses: D. C. Morrison, John Day

Recorded 18 Mar 1851

Book D, P 362
Know all men that I have sold to James G. Stroop a girl slave named
Matilda, 5, for $250.
17 Mar 1851   Thomas J. Stewart
Witnesses: Joseph M. Terry, Thomas J. Peck
Recorded 2 Apr 1851

Book D, P 392
Know ye all men that I, Enoch B. Whitson, have sold to Solomon
Feazel, a negro woman named Sydna, 30, for $700.
7 Apr 1851   E. B. Whitson
                                    Solomon Feazel
Witnesses: M. B. Cooper, J. R. Parker
Recorded 9 Apr 1851

Book D, P 397
Know ye all men that I, Martin Mims, have sold to A. Armstrong, a
negro slave named Ellick, 28, for $1600.
10 May 1851   Martin Mims
                                    Archibald Armstrong
Witnesses: B. F. Dillard, H. Regenburg
Recorded 10 May 1851

Book D, P 406
Know ye all men that I have sold to Colvin Y. Norman the following
slaves: Dinah, 40, and her children, Harrison, 10, Julia, 9, Parthena, 6,
Lewis, 4, and Will, 2, for $1800.
24 Mar 1851   Coatney L. Norman
                                    Colvin Y. Norman
Witnesses: J. J. Daniel, Samuel L. Wright
Recorded 7 Apr 1851

Book D, P 408
In consideration of the love and affection I have for him, I have given
to my son, Joseph Baker, the following slaves. Peter, 55, his wife,
Cherry, 50, and their children, Bill and Ben, and an infant. (No ages
shown.)

4 Mar 1847   Rebecca Baker
Witnesses: Charles Lapster, John Weaver (Deed was executed in Autauga County, Alabama, recorded in Union Parish 24 Apr 1851)

Book D, P 418
I, Thomas Pearson, acknowledge that I have sold to John A. Bayless a negro slave named Joe, 12, for $575.
20 May 1857   Thos Pearson
                               Jno A. Bayless
Witnesses: G. A. Hammond, E. B. Whitson
Recorded 24 May 1857

Book D, P 438
Know ye all men by these presents that I have sold to Joseph B. Matthews a slave named Henry, 15, for $950.
16 Aug 1849   Wilkes Ramsey
                               Joseph B. Matthews
Witnesses: W. S. McGough, H. P. Anderson
Recorded 7 Nov 1851

Book D, P 449
Before me, Reuben Ellis, Notary Public, came William T. H. Manning who declares he sold to Benjamin B. West, for $1600, 4 slaves, Harry, 14, Emily, 13, Jefferson, 11, and Major, 9.
27 Aug 1850   W. T. H. Manning
                               B. B. West
Witnesses: W. H. McFarland, Thomas Van Hook
Recorded 27 Aug 1850

Book D, P 483
Know ye all men that I, Williamson Milburn, have this date sold to Elias George a negro woman named Rachel, 25, for $1200.
7 Aug 1851   Williamson Milburn
                               Elias George
Witnesses: John Marsh, William Merrill
Recorded 7 Aug 1851

Book D, P 483

Know all men that I, James M. Turner, have sold to Henry C. Turner, a man, Jeff, 45, a boy, Foster, 16, and a girl, Sarah, 14, for $1400.

16 Aug 1851   James M. Turner
                              Henry C. Turner

Witnesses: N. Betterton, Henry Regenburg
Recorded 16 Aug 1851

Book D, P 514
Know ye all men that I, William Chapman, of Union County, Arkansas, have sold to Ben B. West two slaves, Madison, 8, and Martha, 32, for $1000.

18 Oct 1851   W. Chapman
                              B. B. West

Witnesses: A. H. Lockhart, O. G. Davis
Recorded 18 Oct 1851

Book D, P 539
Know ye that I have sold to Ann Taylor a man, Wiley, 21, and a girl, Phillis, 12, for $1100.

6 Mar 1850   Jemima Crawford
Witnesses: G. W. Bearden, Joseph W. Terry
Recorded 5 Nov 1851

Book D, P 541
Know ye all men by these presents that I, Benjamin W. West, have sold to Reuben Ellis for $1350, the slaves Martha, 35, and a boy, 8. (No name shown.)

16 Oct 1851   Benjamin W. West
                              Reuben Ellis

Witnesses: H. Regenburg, C. T. Barton
Recorded 4 Nov 1851

Book D, P 544
In consideration of the sum of $780, I have sold to James C. Manning a slave boy, Valentine, 15.

21 Nov 1851   J. H. Pool
                              James C. Manning

Witnesses: Eli Collins, H. Payne
Recorded 21 Nov 1851

Book D, P 560
Know ye all men that I have sold to B. B. West a slave girl named
Emily, 18, for $650.
16 Oct 1851   Reuben Ellis
                                         B. B. West
Witness: H. Regenberg
Recorded 16 Oct 1851

Book D, P 561
Know all men that I have sold to Thomas Van Hook a slave named
Littleton, 40, for $900.
8 Dec 1851   George Lambright
                                         Thos. Van Hook
Witness: H. Bailey
Recorded 8 Dec 1851

Book D, P 567
Know ye all men that I, Wm. M. Lawrence, administrator of the estate
of Timothy Crane, deceased, have sold to Solomon Feazel a negro
woman named Winney and her son, Aleck, for $775. (No ages
shown.)
25 Nov 1851   Wm. M. Lawrence
                                         Solomon Feazel
Witnesses: W. J. Ball, N. M. Bryan
Recorded 29 Nov 1851

Book D, P 584
Before me, Reuben Ellis, Parish Recorder, appeared William A.
Glasson and Harriett Glasson, his wife, who state they have sold to
James E. Jones a negro slave named Phill, 19, for $950.
19 Feb 1852   William A. Glasson
                                         Harriett A. Glasson
                                         James E. Jones
Witnesses: G. W. Sims, William Culverhouse
Recorded 19 Feb 1852

Book D, P 609

Received of Hugh Yongue the sum of $1000 for a slave named Bob, 23.

12 Mar 1852   Casandra L. Smith
                                     Luke H. Smith
                                     Hugh Yongue
Witnesses: William O. Jones, H. Taylor
Recorded 12 Mar 1852

Book D, P 610
Before me, Reuben Ellis, Notary Public, appeared Fergurson Haile, who declares he has sold to W. R. Mayo, a negro slave named Bill, 21, for $1000.

4 Feb 1852   Fergurson Haile
                                     W. R. Mayo
Witnesses: W. C. Glasson, Joseph Baker
Recorded 12 Mar 1852

Book D, P 619
Know ye all men that I have sold to Arrena Pettitt for $500 a slave girl named Mary, 13.

17 Apr 1852   Abosolem Wood,
                                     Union County, Arkansas
                                     Arrena Pettitt
Witness: J. C. Kelly
Recorded 17 Apr 1852

Book E, P 5
Received of T. T. Ratliff the sum of $1800, payment for a slave man named Simon, 20.

18 Sep 1850   George W. Honeycutt
                                     Thomas T. Ratliff
Witnesses: H. R. Bryan, H. Regenburg
Recorded 18 Sep 1850

Book E, P 17
Before me, B. E. Ellis, Notary Public, came I. A. R. Van Hook and his wife, Martha J. Van Hook, who declare they sold to John R. Parker and J. G. Hollis certain slaves, to wit, Nancy, 30, Caroline, 14, and Molly, 21, and her son, Anderson, for $2800.

5 Feb 1851   I. A. R. Van Hook
                                           Martha Jane Wood Van Hook
                                           J. R. Parker
                                           J. G. Hollis
Witnesses: Isaac Newton, Nicholas F. White
Recorded 5 Feb 1851

Book E, P 28
Before me, Reuben Ellis, Parish Recorder, appeared Asa Thomas who
declared he sold to James A. Dozier the following slaves. Jim, 40, for
$1900, and Mariah, 25, for $700.
13 Feb 1851   Asa Thomas
                                           James A. Dozier
Witnesses: Eli L. Collins, W. A. McFarland
Recorded 2 Mar 1852

Book E, P 34
This contract of sale made between Needham M. Bryan of first part
and W. O. Jones of second part, first party declaring he sold to party
of second part for $2700, negro slaves, to wit, Betty, 20, and children,
Eliza, 5, Phill, 2, and a boy named Wiley, 22.
27 Apr 1851   N. M. Bryan
                                           W. O. Jones
Witnesses: H. R. Bryan, Henry Lassiter
Recorded 27 Apr 1851

Book E, P 51
Personally appeared before me, Reuben Ellis, Parish Recorder, Henry
R. Bryan, who states he sold to James E. Jones 2 negro slaves, Prince,
38, and Virginia, 13, for $600.
20 May 1851   Henry R. Bryan
                                           James E. Jones
Witnesses: James King, M. McFarland
Recorded 20 May 1851

Book E, P 127
Know ye all men that I have sold to George W. Tubb certain slaves,
Viny, 24, and her child, Jemima, 1; Emily, 22, and her child, Miles, 15
months; and Ned, 17.

12 Mar 1852   M. Ikard
                                        George W. Tubb
Witnesses: H. B. Essick, James King
Recorded 13 Mar 1852

Book E, P 131
Before me, Reuben Ellis, Parish Recorder, came Sarah Martin who
states she has sold to Henry Regenburg a slave named Girsella, 22, and
her 2 children. (No ages or values shown.)
19 Mar 1852   Sarah Martin
                                        H. Regenburg
Witnesses: B. B. West, George W. Sims
Recorded 24 Mar 1852

Book E, P 133
In consideration of the sum of $126, I, Johnson Malone, due to my
indebtedness to Archibald Armstrong, for the purpose of securing the
final payment I hereby mortgage Hall, about 13, a negro slave boy.
11 Dec 1857   Johnson Malone (his mark: X)
                                        Archibald Armstrong
Witnesses: Thomas Van Hook, James A. Dozier
Recorded 11 Dec 1857

Book E, P 139
Be it known that before me, H. B. Cenas, Notary Public for the city
and parish of New Orleans, appeared James Moore who states he has
sold to Samuel J. Larkin 4 negro slaves, to wit, Major, 31, Jack, 19,
Munroe, 17, and (name obscure, 13), for the sum of $1428.50.
4 May 1852   James Moore
                                        S. J. Larkin
Witnesses: A. Commander, Charles Barry (Deed was executed in New
Orleans, recorded in Union Parish 5 May 1852).

Book E, P 147
Before me, William Shannon, Notary Public, came Larkin C.
Callaway, who states that for the sum of $1500 he has sold to Purvis
Wood certain slaves, Martha, 17, Mary, 40, Easter, 30, Henry, 25, and
Solomon, 14.
27 Apr 1852   L. C. Callaway

Purvis Wood

Witnesses: Robert T. J. Baker, Robert Pelau (Deed was made in New Orleans, recorded in Union Parish 27 Apr 1852)

Book E, P 195
Before me, D. Pucket, Notary Public, came John M. Crawford, who states he has sold a slave named Jack, 50, for $460.50, property of David Stewart, deceased, to John M. Cranford.
23 Mar 1853   John M. Crawford
                                     John M. Cranford
Witnesses: David A. Phillips, I. A. R. Van Hook
Recorded 23 Mar 1853

Book E, P 228
Before me, Reuben Ellis, came Larkin C. Callaway, who declares he sold to John Stow 2 slaves, Warner, 30, and Hetty, a woman, 22. (No value shown.)
7 Dec 1853   L. C. Callaway
                                     John Stow
Witnesses: John Young, J. G. Taylor
Recorded 7 Dec 1853

Book E, P 230
Know all men that I have sold to Thomas A. Rains a slave man named Warren, 30, for $1500.
16 Dec 1853   John Stow
                                     T. A. Rains
Witnesses: Hiram Peevey, Frederick Rains
Recorded 16 Dec 1853

Book E, P 233
Pursuant to order of the 12th Judicial Court, I have sold at auction slaves of the estate of C. B. Jones, deceased. To William A. Glasson, Flora, 35, Stepney, a girl, 2, and Susan, 6, for $1660. To Hugh Yongue, Pink, a woman, 30, for $1000. To Elizabeth Y. Hester, Prissilla, 10, for $505. To W. J. Q. Baker, Affrey, a woman, 15, and Stephen, 28, for $1500.
12 Feb 1853   David B. Trousdale, Sheriff
Witnesses: H. B. Essick, E. M. Jarman

Recorded 24 Dec 1853

Book E, P 248
In consideration of the sum of $800, I have sold to Alex Shlenker a
slave man, Israel, 25, for $800.
20 Feb 1854   W. O. Jones
                              Alex Shlenker
Witnesses: Henry March, H. Regenburg
Recorded 20 Feb 1854

Book E, P 251
Pursuant to an order of the 12th Judicial Court, I, Louisa C. Rimes,
have sold to Silas Phillips at auction for $500 a negro slave named
Wilson (age not shown), property of the estate of John D. Rimes,
deceased.
28 Dec 1853   Louisa C. Rimes, adm
Witness: H. Regenburg
Recorded 8 Mar 1854

Book E, P 254
As decreed by the 12th Judicial Court, I, Arrena Thompson,
administrator of the estate of William B. Thompson, deceased, have
sold to highest bidders at auction, slaves of the estate as follows: to
Royal K. Love, Luck, a man, for $1590. To Archibald Armstrong,
Mitchel, for $1425. To W. B. Norsworthy, Caleb, for $1815. To N. D.
M. Bruton, Bill, for $1000 and Matilda, for $1100. To Samuel Smith,
Sharlott, for $1525. To James A. Creath, Emily and her child, for
$1405. To T. M. McFadin, Rachel and child for $1330. To V. I. Bird,
Milly, for $1550. To James Pettit, Dorkis, a woman for $810 (ages of
slaves not shown).
10 Feb 1854   Arrena Thompson
Witnesses: John C. Kelly, Henry Phelps
Recorded 17 Mar 1854

Book E, P 265
Know ye all men that I, William O. Jones, have sold to Hugh Yongue,
a slave girl, Ann, 25, for $410.
18 May 1854   W. O. Jones
                              H. Yongue

Witnesses: Allen Carr, S. Shepherd
Recorded 18 May 1854

Book E, P 287
Pursuant to an order of the 12th Judicial Court, I, Thomas Brantley, have sold at auction the slave Henry, 24, for $1200, to Elizabeth Brantley, the highest bidder.
22 Jan 1855   Thos Brantley
Witnesses: W. T. Tisdale, S. N. Smith
Recorded 22 Jan 1855

Book E, P 297
Know ye all men that I, James Moore, have sold to Williams, Phillips and Company, for $2570, slaves, to wit, John, 26, Chesby, 24, Major, 22, and Sump, 18, all brothers.
14 Feb 1855   Jas. Moore
Witnesses: Nicholas Johnson, Everett Pettipaw (Deed was executed in New Orleans, recorded in Union Parish 14 Feb 1855.)

Book E, P 309
Before me, William C. Smith, Parish Recorder, came James Hart who declares he has sold to Wright, Davenport and Co., of New Orleans, following slaves (ages and value not shown): Hannah, Charles, Davis, Louisa, William, Exena, Nancy, Abram, Watt, Dick, Linda, Rachel, Eliza, Dianna, Priss, Lewis, Henry, Willis, Daniel, Little Watt, Sandy, Ellick, Marge, Sam, Anna, Betsey, Rossette, Solomon, Gust, Stepney, Phillip, Harvey, Lane, Bunch, Tom, Violet, Humphrey, Frank, Sarah, Ben, Ruth, Martha, Polly and her child, Eliza and her child, Winney and her child, Fanny and her children, Stephen and Egbert; and Silvey, a girl.
24 Apr 1855   James Hart
                                           James A. Creath, Agent for
                                           Wright, Davenport and Co.
Witnesses: James Moore, James D. Johnson
Recorded 24 Apr 1855

Book E, P 348
Pursuant to an order of the 12th Judicial Court, I, Wiley Underwood, have sold at auction to highest bidders slaves of the estate of Aaron M.

Jones, deceased. To Wiley Underwood for $2395, Clara and children, Ally, John, Charles, Jina and Isaac; to George Killgore for $1200, Lige, a man, and William, for $950; to George W. Goodwin for $905, Louinda; to Washington J. Pickel, for $1050, Matt. (No ages shown.)
2 Jun 1855   Wiley Underwood
Witnesses: R. G. Pleasant, W. J. Larkin
Recorded 6 Aug 1855

Book E, P 365
By order of the 12th Judicial Court, I, William H. Dixon, administrator of the estate of Mixon D. Dixon, deceased, have sold to the highest bidders at auction the following slaves. Cela, 36, to John Culbertson for $700. Caesar, 20, to E. R. Milner for $1375. Martha, 22, to William White for $1003.
2 Nov 1855   William H. Dixon
Witnesses: Robert J. Caldwell, John L. Barrett
Recorded 13 Nov 1855

Book E, P 382
By order of the 12th Judicial Court, I sold at auction to highest bidder, Geo W. Murphy, a negro slave named Hiram, 20, for $1305, property of the estate of Samuel Montgomery, deceased.
1 Mar 1856   Wiley Underwood, adm
Witness: F. Haile
Recorded 19 Mar 1856

Book E, P 387
By order of the 12th Judicial Court, I, Cullen Edwards, administrator of the estate of Thomas M. Hand, dec'd, sold at auction slaves of the estate as indicated. To Robert N. Richardson, Easter, 27, for $1075. To Ferguson Haile, Willis, 21, for $1360. To Elijah Miller, Antony, for $1200. To H. C. Glasson, Ned, 58, for $683.
21 Dec 1855   Cullen Edwards
Witnesses: John L. Barrett, S. O. Larche
Recorded 1 Feb 1856

Book E, P 392
We, John P. Everett and B. W. Brown, administrators of the estate of George Everett, deceased, proceeded to sell slaves of the estate, by

order of the 12th Judicial Court. To highest cash bidders the following slaves were sold. To B. W. Brown, Sam, about 30, his wife, Rose, and their children, Harriett, 9, Allen 5, Pleasant, 3, and Joshua, 2, for $3400. To James Moore, Caroline, 21, and her children, Bina and Sarah (ages not shown) for $1700. To H. M. Tubb, Milley, 38, and her child Elijah for $1020. To Gideon H. Burke, Patience, 43, and her child, Hannah, 9, for $1030. To David B. Briggs, Judy, 45, for $600. To M. Johnson, Aleck, 27, for $1400. To J. P. Everett, Joe, 21, for $1460. To G. W. Everett, Jim, 70, for $100.

15 Jan 1856   John P. Everett
                         B. W. Brown
Witnesses: (names obscure)
Recorded 15 Jan 1856

Book F, P 8
Before me, Reuben Ellis, Notary Public, came John G. Kelley who states he has sold to Elizabeth Ann Green, wife of Solomon Powell, a slave girl, Rachel, 16, for $600.

30 Apr 1852   John G. Kelley
                         E. Ann Powell
Witnesses: James Pettit, Charles Absent
Recorded 30 Apr 1852

Book F, P 14
Know ye all men that I, Valin I. Bird, in consideration of the sum of $1000, have sold to Jordan G. Taylor, the following slaves: Margaret, (no age shown) and Tom, 11.

13 Feb 1852   Valin I. Bird
                         Jordan G. Taylor
Witnesses: Allen Carr, W. H. Carr
Recorded 30 Apr 1852

Book F, P 38
Personally came before me, Reuben Ellis, Parish Recorder, Wilkes Ramsey, L. W. Ramsey, G. W. Ramsey, H. W. Ramsey, James Ramsey, Mary Ramsey, John Ramsey, D. B. Ramsey, and C. L. Ramsey, who declare they have sold to Malcomb McFarland, the surviving husband of Mary Ramsey, deceased, a certain slave, property

of the estate of James Ramsey, deceased, named Mahala, 10. (Value not shown.)

10 Jan 1851   M. McFarland, grantee

Witnesses: D. R. Delk, W. A. Glasson
Recorded 8 May 1852

Book F, P 39

Before me, Reuben Ellis, Parish Recorder, personally came L. W. Ramsey, H. W. Ramsey, John Ramsey, D. B. Ramsey, G. W. Ramsey, Malcomb McFarland, and James Ramsey, who declare they have sold to Humphrey W. R. Ramsey a negro girl, Ann, property of the estate of James Ramsey, deceased. (Value not shown.)

31 Dec 1851   Humphrey W. R. Ramsey,
                                               grantee

Witnesses: E. J. Barton, W. A. Glasson
Recorded 7 May 1852

Book F, P 44

Know ye all men that I, Elijah Tabor, have sold to W. A. Glasson, certain negro slaves, Phillis, 28, and her children, Thor, a boy, 6, Peter, 2, and Virginia, infant, for $900.

10 May 1852   Elijah Tabor
                                               W. A. Glasson

Witnesses: William Culverhouse, M. D. Mayes
Recorded 10 May 1852

Book F, P 53

Know ye all men that I, D. B. Trousdale, Sheriff, sold at auction to Eliza Barton a negro man named Lorenzo, 25, formerly property of M. T. Ellis, for $900.

5 Apr 1852   David B. Trousdale
                                               Eliza Barton

Witness: E. C. Russell
Recorded 13 May 1852

Book F, P 56

Know all men by these presents that I have sold to John Sterling a slave girl named Judy, 14, for $700.

5 Nov 1850   Henry B. Lassiter

John Sterling
Witnesses: N. M. Bryan, Daniel Payne
Recorded 14 May 1852

Book F, P 71
In consideration of the affection I have for him, I, Joseph M. Warren, have given to Jasper Warren a slave boy named Izaah, 8.
9 Sep 1852   Joseph M. Warren
                                   Jasper Warren
Witnesses: Abner Green, Sarah Warren
Recorded 9 Sep 1852

Book F, P 92
Know ye all men that I have this day swopt (sic) my negro man Stephen to my sister Rhody H. Hines for her negro woman, Mariah, both got by our father's estate. (No ages shown.)
1 Feb 1852   Jesse W. Glass
Witness: Joel Glass (Deed was executed in Neshoba County, Mississippi, recorded in Union Parish 1 Feb 1852).

Book F, P 93
Before me, D. Puckett, Notary Public, came William D. Cooper who states he has sold to Liberty K. Thomas a slave woman named Caroline, 22, and her child, Samuel (no age shown) for $700.
5 Jun 1852   William D. Cooper
                                   Liberty K. Thomas
Witnesses: R. May, Marshall Day
Recorded 10 Jul 1852

Book F, P 157
Know ye all men that, in consideration of the sum of $700, we, John H. Hines and Rhoda Hines have sold to G. W. Sims one negro slave named Catherine. (No age shown.)
15 Oct 1852   John H. Hines
                                   Rhoda Hines
                                   G. W. Sims
Witnesses: J. Y. Henderson, W. A. Glasson
Recorded 16 Oct 1852

Book F, P 188
Know ye that we, Hugh C. Glasson and James A. Taylor have exchanged the following slaves: Anderson, 9, formerly owned by J. A. Taylor, to H. C. Glasson in exchange for his slave, Charlotte, 8.
2 Nov 1852   H. C. Glasson
                                    James A. Taylor
Witnesses: D. B. Trousdale, H. B. Essick
Recorded 20 Dec 1952

Book F, P 202
By order of the 12th Judicial Court, I, James Gresham, administrator of the estate of Mary Jane Masterson, deceased, have sold at auction to highest bidder (McDuel Bilberry), viz, Tumer, a boy, 17, for $1100.
30 Oct 1852   James Gresham
                                    McDuel Bilberry
Witnesses: John B. Robinson, J. G. Bilberry
Recorded 17 Jan, 1853

Book F, P 203
In consideration of the natural love I have for Emily Ann Callaway, wife of Wm G. Callaway, I have given to her for the sum of 1 dollar a negro named Silas, 11.
21 May 1852   Frances Callaway
                                    Emily A. Callaway
Witnesses: Benjamin J. Driver, B. Moore
Recorded 19 Jan 1853

Book F, P 222
Received at Farmerville in the State of Louisiana of James S. Carson and John A. Bayless the sum of $1000, as payment for a negro slave named Wallace, 26.
6 Jan 1853   Thomas M. Hand
                                    John A. Bayless
                                    James S. Carson
Witnesses: G. A. Hammock, M. S. Carson
Recorded 10 Feb 1853

Book F, P 223

Know all men that I, William O. Jones, have sold to C. B. Jones a negro man named Stephen (no age shown) for the sum of $1500.

8 Feb 1853   William O. Jones
                                   C. B. Jones

Witnesses: W. A. Glasson, H. Regenburg
Recorded 11 Feb 1853

Book F, P 227
Pursuant to order of the 12th Judicial Court, I, Martin Hendrick, sold at auction slaves of the estate of William T. H. Manning, decd, to wit, Harry, 18, to William Ham, for $1575. Major, 11, to John Odom, for $700.

12 Feb 1853   Martin Hendrick, adm

Witnesses: W. H. Carson, H. B. Essick
Recorded 21 Feb 1853

Book F, P 231
Received of James Jones $600 in payment for a slave woman named Hilda, 30.

28 Feb 1853   Cassandra Smith
                                   J. Jones

Witnesses: Ralph Jones (his mark: X), J. E. Jones
Recorded 28 Feb 1853

Book F, P 242
Before me, Daniel Pucket, Notary Public, came David A. Phillips, to declare he sold to Henry Phelps a slave girl named Mary, 20, for $600.

4 Mar 1853   David A. Phillips
                                   Henry Phelps

Witnesses: I. A. R. Van Hook, Uriah Bass
Recorded 8 Mar 1853

Book F, P 247
Know ye that I, Wm. J. Goyne, administrator of the estate of Hiram D. Goyne, deceased, have sold to Joseph Baker, the negro man Bill, 27, for the sum of $1056.

29 Dec 1852   Wm. J. Goyne
                                   Joseph Baker

Witnesses: Thomas Van Hook, B. H. Petersen

Recorded 17 Mar 1853

Book F, P 257
Know ye all men that I have sold to Pinkney Odom a slave woman
named Lucy, 35, for $500.
11 Apr 1853   Elijah M. Aulds
                                     Pinkney Odom
Witnesses: John Boatright, James L. Patton
Recorded 11 Apr 1853

Book F, P 258
Know ye that we, James A. Coleson and wife have sold to Alexander
M. Taylor a female slave of 10 years, named Charity, for $500.
21 Jan 1853   James A. Coleson
                                     Prudentia Coleson (her mark: X)
Witnesses: F. M. Armstrong, Josiah Hill
Recorded 11 Apr 1853

Book F, P 270
Before me, D. Puckett, Notary Public, came John Traylor who
declares he sold to Thomas J. Stewart, certain slaves, Betsey, 36, and
her child (No name shown.); Tyler, 12, Eveline, 8, John Michel, 5, and
Esther, 3.
14 Apr 1853   John Traylor
                                     Thomas J. Stewart
Witnesses: S. D. Mims, Richard Bass
Recorded 22 Apr 1853

Book F, P 274
Know all men that I, Rebecca P. Phelps, have sold to Paschal B.
Traylor for $3000, slaves of the estate of Henry Phelps, deceased, to
wit, Tom, 40, Mandy, 17, and Jane, 20, and her son, Daniel, 2.
21 Apr 1853   Rebecca P. Phelps
                                     P. B. Traylor
Witnesses: H. Regenburg, J. H. Traylor
Recorded 21 Apr 1853

Book F, P 291

Before me, Reuben Ellis, Parish Recorder, came Asa Thomas who declares he has sold to W. W. Farmer a negro woman named Maria, 40, for $500.

23 Jun 1853   Asa Thomas
                                     W. W. Farmer

Witnesses: B. M. Rimes, C. T. Barton
Recorded 24 Jun 1853

Book F, P 304
Before me, Daniel Puckett, Notary Public, came Wiley Underwood and his wife, Ann M. Jones, who state they have sold to Charles C. Hand and his wife, Sarah Underwood, certain slaves, for $6250, viz, Charles, 25, Catherine, 12, Abel, 27, Palina, 23, and her child, Ellen, 9, and Betsey, 25, and her son, Jim. (No age shown.)

16 Jul 1853   W. Underwood
                                     Charles C. Hand

Witnesses: H. Regenburg, J. M. Underwood
Recorded 30 Aug 1853

Book F, P 319
Before me, Reuben Ellis, Notary Public, came H. C. Glasson who states he has sold to V. I. Bird a negro boy named Andy, 10, for $800.

5 Sep 1853   H. C. Glasson
                                     V. I. Bird

Witnesses: Ferguson Haile, B. W. Rimes
Recorded 14 Sep 1853

Book F, P 329
Know ye all men by these presents that I, Thomas M. Hand, in consideration of the sum of $600, have sold to James C. Manning my slave girl, Mary, 11.

7 Sep 1853   T. M. Hand
                                     James C. Manning

Witnesses: H. B. Essick, W. H. Carson
Recorded 24 Sep 1853

Book F, P 348

Before me, D. Puckett, Notary Public, came William B. McCaleb, who declares he has sold for $600 a slave boy, Washington, to William Parrott.

10 Jan 1853   W. B. McCaleb
                                     William Parrott
Witnesses: James Russell, Charles R. Dennis
Recorded 17 Nov 1853

Book F, P 352
Know ye all men by these presents that in consideration of the love and affection I have for my son, William H. Culbertson, I, John Culbertson, convey to the said William H. Culbertson two negro boys, John, 12, and Hue, 10, and give to my daughter, Mary J. Gill, a negro girl named Hulda, 7.

20 Jul 1853   John Culbertson
                                     Mary J. Gill
                                     Wm H. Culbertson
Witnesses: W. J. Raney, C. H. Dacus
Recorded 21 Nov 1853

Book F, P 356
Be it known that for the love and affection I have for them, I have given to my children slaves as indicated. To my son, Daniel Frederick Rester, Peter, 2; to my son, Francis Marion Rester, Franklin, 4; to my daughter, Sarah Rester, Hannah, 4, and Henry, 5; to my son, William Rester, George, 7; to my son, Liberty Rester, James, 6; to my daughter, Mary Jane Rester, Manda, 7 months; to my son, Gideon Rester, Martha, 30; and to Albert Hezekiah Rester, my son, Harriett, 30 (value of slaves not shown).

27 Nov 1853   Hezekiah Rester
Witness: Oliver Bryan Hill, Notary Public
Recorded 28 Nov 1853

Book F, P 419
Know all men by these presents that I, L. C. Callaway, in consideration of the sum of $1500, have sold to T. A. Rains a negro slave named Warren, about 30 years old.

16 Dec 1853   L. C. Callaway
                                     T. A. Rains

Witnesses: F. Rains, D. L. Hicks
Recorded 16 Dec 1853

Book F, P 430
Know ye all men by these presents that I, V. I. Bird, have sold to
Lazarus Brunner, for the sum of $400, a negro woman named Penney,
45.
11 Jan 1854   V. I. Bird
                                      L. Brunner
Witnesses: Alex Shlenker, H. March
Recorded 11 Jan 1854

Book F, P 431
In consideration of the sum of $850, I, W. W. Farmer, have sold to
Alexander Shlenker, a negro slave woman, aged about 40, named
Maria.
6 Jan 1854   W. W. Farmer (his mark: X)
                                      Alex Shlenker
Witnesses: H. B. Essick, H. Regenburg
Recorded 11 Jan 1854

Book F, P 431
Know all ye men that I have sold to Louis Mayer a slave woman
named Maria, 40, for the sum of $650.
6 Jan 1854   W. W. Farmer (his mark: X)
                                      Louis Mayer
Witnesses: H. B. Essick, H. Regenburg
Recorded 11 Jan 1854

Book F, P 432
Know ye all men by these presents that for the sum of $800, I have
sold to Sylvanus Shepherd a negro slave named Andy, 12.
4 Apr 1854   Valin I Bird
                                      Sylvanus Shepherd
Witnesses: Ferguson Haile, J. G. Taylor
Recorded 12 Oct 1854

Book F, P 433

Know ye all men that for the sum of $1250, I, V. I. Bird, have sold to Sylvanus Shepherd 3 negro slaves: Betty, 35, and her children, Grady, 6, and Dianna, 3.

12 Jan 1854   V. I. Bird
                                    Sylvanus Shepherd

Witnesses: D. R. Delk, Allen Carr
Recorded 12 Jan 1854

Book F, P 439
Be it remembered that I, Wm. A. Milner, by order of the 12th Judicial Court, have sold at auction to John A. Bayless and James H. Carson, a slave of the estate of Hugh Ivey, deceased, Lewis, 23, for $1170.

12 Jan 1854   Wm. A. Milner
Witnesses: Moses S. Carson, D. A. Bryan
Recorded 20 Jan 1854

Book F, P 440
Received of John A. Bayless in full payment for a slave named Joe, 21, the sum of $1500.

20 Jan 1854   Thomas Van Hook
                                    John A. Bayless

Witnesses: Moses S. Carson, James D. Slawson
Recorded 20 Jan 1854

Book F, P 440
Be it known that in consideration of the love and affection I have for my daughter, Louisa A. Gaskill, I have given to her certain negro slaves, to wit, Ned and his wife, Hannah, and their children, William, Sykes, and Charlotte Elizabeth, and a negro girl named Ann. (No ages shown.)

20 Jan 1854   John W. Kidd
                                    Louisa A. Gaskill

Witness: J. V. McGrane, Justice of the Peace (Deed was executed in Shelby County, Alabama, recorded in Union Parish 25 Jan 1854).

Book G, P 4
Know ye all men that I have sold to James Matthews a negro girl named Charity, 12, for $700.

13 Feb 1854   Alex M. Taylor

105

James Matthews
Witnesses: John Taylor, William Taylor
Recorded 17 Feb 1854

Book G, P 7
Received of Amanda Norris the sum of $800, payment for a slave boy
named Hibonette, 11.
1 Feb 1854   John Wright
                                             Amanda Norris
Witnesses: J. G. Wright, Thomas M. Wright
Recorded 14 Feb 1854

Book G, P 16
Know ye that I have sold to Hugh Yongue a slave man named Israel,
27, for $1000.
6 Mar 1854   W. O. Jones
                                             H. Yongue
Witnesses: H. Regenberg, Alex Shlenker
Recorded 7 Mar 1854

Book G, P 26
In consideration of the affection I bear him, I have sold to my son,
Andrew T. Matthews, for the sum of $100, a negro boy named Peter,
10.
4 Feb 1854   John Matthews
                                             Andrew T. Matthews
Witnesses: Oliver B. Hill, F. Brazzel
Recorded 4 Apr 1854

Book G, P 41
Received of John Odom the sum of $1100, in payment for a slave boy
named Majer, 37.
27 Mar 1854   B. B. West
                                             John Odom

Witness: D. A. Darby
Recorded 8 May 1854

Book G, P 42

Before me, William C. Smith, Parish Recorder, appeared Casandra L. Smith who states she has sold a slave, a boy named Verg, 10, for $600, to James Jones.

3 May 1854   Casandra L. Smith
                             J. Jones

Witnesses: B. B. West, Thos Van Hook
Recorded 10 May 1854

Book G, P 43
Know ye all men that I, Jesse Fuller, have sold to James E. Jones a negro man named Shadrick (age not shown) for $1200.

11 May 1854   J. G. Fuller
                             James E. Jones

Witnesses: Allen Carr, W. A. Darby
Recorded 11 May 1854

Book G, P 45
Know all men by these presents that I have sold to Eliza Ann Rossiter a slave man named Kane, 30, for $1300.

14 Jan 1854   Robert C. Webb Jr
                             Eliza Ann Rossiter

Witnesses: S. A. Auld, W. C. Smith
Recorded 22 May 1854

Book G, P 46
Know ye all men that I, William O. Jones, have sold to Hugh Yongue slaves as follows: Ann, 25, Pheba, 10, Marina, 8, Candis, 6, Tom, 2, and Steve, 12, for total sum of $1036.

26 May 1854   W. O. Jones
                             H. Yongue

Witnesses: H. B. Essick, J. G. Taylor
Recorded 26 May 1854

Book G, P 53
In consideration of the love and affection I have for my daughter, Jane L. Kilgore, now wife of Anderson Fleming, I have given to her negro slaves: Pinney, a woman, 26, Rose, 21, and her child, Frances, 2, and Edny, a girl, 8.

7 Jan 1853   Julia A. Kilgore

Jane L. Fleming
Witness: John Hollis, Justice of the Peace (Deed was executed in Ashley County, Alabama, recorded in Union Parish 28 Jan 1853).

Book G, P 54
Know ye all men that I, James Watkins, have sold for the sum of $1000 to Peter R. Goldsby a negro girl named Mille, 26.
10 Jan 1854   James Watkins
                                               Peter R. Goldsby
Witnesses. G. W. Murphy, James Moore
Recorded 12 Jul 1854

Book G, P 60
Know all men by these presents that I have sold to Eliza Ann Rossiter a slave man named Green, 38, for $1200.
25 Jul 1854   James W. Coleson
                                               Eliza Ann Rossiter
Witnesses: W. F. Crawford, W. H. Rossiter
Recorded 11 Aug 1854

Book G, P 66
Rec'd of Miss F. M. Norman, payment for a slave man named Andy, 28, the sum of $800.
25 Aug 1854   John Edwards
                                               F. M. Norman
Witnesses: John E. Tay, P. Roan
Recorded 25 Aug 1854

Book G, P 68
Know ye all men by these presents that I, J. E. Green, have sold to J. H. Green for the sum of $4500, negro slaves: Eliza and children, Sara, Sam, Peter, and Liserve. (No ages shown.)
2 Sep 1854   J. E. Green
                                               J. H. Green
Witnesses: D. P. A. Cook, C. T. Barton
Recorded 7 Sep 1854

Book G, P 69

Received of David Ward $1000 in payment for a slave boy named Davis, 20.

7 Sep 1854   Elisha Ward (his mark: X)
                            David Ward

Witnesses: John A. Bayless, Moses Carson
Recorded 7 Sep 1854

Book G, P 94
Know all men by these presents that I, John Matthews, have sold to my son, Francis B. Matthews, for the sum of $200, a negro boy named Isaac, 9.

15 Nov 1854   John Matthews
                          F. B. Matthews

Witnesses: F. Brazzel, Benjamin L. Harrell
Recorded 15 Nov 1854

Book G, P 117
Know all men by these presents that I, John H. Wright, a resident of the state of Arkansas, have sold to V. I. Bird a negro woman named Matilda, 18, and her child, Mariah, 5 months old, for $900.

23 Nov 1854   John H. Wright
                          V. I. Bird

Witnesses: H. B. Essick, M. D. Mayes
Recorded 28 Nov 1854

Book G, P 118
Be it known that I, John W. Ford, have sold to Mary T. Dearing for the sum of $800 a negro boy named Adam. (No age shown.)

24 Feb 1843   John W. Ford
                          Mary T. Dearing

Witness: William J. Capp, Attorney (Deed was executed in Warren County, Tennessee, recorded in Union Parish 24 Feb 1853)

Book G, P 119
Know ye all men that in consideration of the sum of $1000, paid to me, Matthew W. Lindsay, I have sold to Mary T. Dearing, 3 negro slaves, viz, Dick, about 50, Charlotte, about 40, and Jane, 17.

29 Nov 1854   M. W. Lindsay
                          Mary T. Dearing

Witness: J. W. Williams (Deed was executed in Franklin County, Alabama, recorded in Union Parish 29 Nov 1854)

Book G, P 134
Received of W. J. Pickel the sum of $600, payment for a slave girl, Mary, 30.
2 Jan 1855   Solomon Powell
                                        W. J. Pickel
Witness: S. L. Larkin
Recorded 2 Jan 1855

Book G, P 134
In consideration of the love I have for her, I have given my daughter, Amanda Elizabeth Jane Wood, for the sum of 1 dollar, a slave girl, May, 3.
2 Jan 1855   Mary Cole (her mark: X)
                                        Amanda E. Wood
Witnesses: Jeremiah Dubose, Wade H. Dubose (Deed was executed in Pike County, Alabama, recorded in Union Parish 15 Jan 1855.)

Book G, P 135
In consideration of the love I have for her, I have given to my daughter, Jenetta Wood, wife of John Wood, a slave girl named Sopha, and her children, Cely, 5, and Lucinda, 3.
2 Jan 1854   Mary Cole (her mark: X)
                                        Jenetta Wood
Witness: John D. Curtis, County Clerk (Deed was executed in Pike County, Alabama, recorded in Union Parish 10 Jan 1854.)

Book G, P 145
Pursuant to an order of the 12th Judicial Court, I have sold at public auction slaves of the estate of John M. Crawford, deceased, as follows: To Thomas B. Kelly, Jack, 25, for $1440. To James M. Lupo, Caroline and her children, Chany, Westly, and Mary (no ages shown) for $1600. To Hillary H. Ham, Mary for $535. (No age shown.)
26 Dec 1854   L. H. Carson, Deputy Sheriff
Witnesses: F. L. Cook, M. D. Myers
Recorded 8 Jan 1855

Book G, P 165
I, John Hendrick, have sold to John Odom a slave boy named Charles, 32, for $1300, property of estate of Phoebe Hendrick, deceased, by order of the 12th Judicial Court.
23 Jan 1855   John W. Hendrick, adm
                                     John Odom
Witnesses: R. W. Windes, B. W. Odom
Recorded 1 Feb 1855

Book G, P 172
Pursuant to an order of the 12th Judicial Court, I, S. W. Ramsey, administrator of the estate of Henry R. Bryan, deceased, have sold to highest bidder at auction a slave named Prince (age not shown) for $1100 (to Richard Fowler).
3 Feb 1855   S. W. Ramsey
                                     Richard Fowler
Witnesses: Davis Ward, Allen Stansell
Recorded 5 Feb 1855

Book G, P 174
Before me, Wm. C. Smith, Parish Recorder, came Thomas M. Hand, who declares that he has sold to V. I. Bird a negro slave girl named Grace, 13, for the sum of $1000.
7 Feb 1855   Thomas M. Hand
                                     V. I. Bird
Witnesses: M. D. Mays, F. Haile
Recorded 8 Feb 1855

Book G, P 182
Be it known that in consideration of the love and affection I have for my daughter, Nancy Fuller, I, Daniel Payne, have granted to her the following slaves, with a total value of $1200. Ellen, 35, and children, Andy, James, Bolliver, Harris, and Quincy; and Mariah and son, Perry. (Ages not shown.)
17 Feb 1855   Daniel Payne
                                     Nancy Fuller
                                     (wife of Jesse Fuller)
Witnesses: W. M. Reynolds, Jemus Mills

111

Recorded 17 Feb 1855

Book G, P 183
Before me, William C. Smith, Parish Recorder, came Peter R. Golsby, who declares he he sold to John E. Green two negro slaves, Andy, 23, and Clark, 14, for $1500.
17 Feb 1855   P. R. Golsby
                                     John E. Green
Witnesses: W. W. Wassen, Alfred Honeycutt
Recorded 26 Feb 1855

Book G, P 183
Before me, William C. Smith, Parish Recorder, came Harrison E. Whiting, who declares that for the sum of $1000, he has sold to D. G. Temple negro slaves, Polly, 18, and her children, Charlott, 4, and Walter, 7 months.
18 Feb 1855   H. E. Whiting
                                     D. G. Temple
Witness: J. A. White
Recorded 26 Feb 1855

Book G, P 188
Before me, Wm C. Smith, Parish Recorder, came T. M. Hand who declares he has sold to Lewis Reppond a negro slave named Wash, 36, for the sum of $1150.
6 Mar 1855   T. M. Hand
                                     Lewis Reppond (his mark: X)
Witnesses: C. T. Barton, W. W. Todd
Recorded 6 Mar 1855

Book G, P 192
Know all men that I have sold to B. M. Tubb a slave named Allen. (No age or value shown.)
5 Mar 1855   John T. Matthews
                                     B. M. Tubb
Witnesses: John Phelps (his mark: X), T. B. Matthews
Recorded 22 Mar 1855

Book G, P 193

Know ye that we have sold to Daniel Payne for $3900 the following slaves: Elic, a boy, 22; Biley, a man, 20; Jesey, a boy, 10, Fox, a boy, 12, and Lucy, 16.

3 Feb 1849   Hugh Yongue
                                       Delaware S. Yongue
Witnesses: H. R. Bryan, W. O. Jones
Recorded 3 Feb 1849

Book G, P 194
Received of Daniel Payne the sum of $700, in payment for a negro boy named Ben. (No age shown.)

23 Mar 1855   W. O. Jones
                                       Daniel Payne
Witness: William C. Smith
Recorded 23 Mar 1855

Book G, P 200
Know all men that I, James Watkins, have sold to William W. Wasson certain slaves for $1300, viz, Barbery, 23, and her son, Samuel, 5.

11 Apr 1855   James Watkins
                                       W. W. Wasson
Witnesses: B. W. Brown, James Moore
Recorded 11 Apr 1855

Book G, P 202
Before me, William C. Smith, Parish Recorder, came George W. Sims who states he has sold to James M. Underwood a slave woman named Catherine, for $1193.

11 Apr 1855   G. W. Sims
                                       J. M. Underwood
Witnesses: R. R. Love, W. C. Smith
Recorded 12 Apr 1855

Book G, P 208
Know all men that I, Robert H. Andrews, have sold to John T. Roberts, for $1300, slaves, to wit, Mariah, 36, Nancy, 11, Emily, 8, Eliza, 6, and Henry, 4.

10 Jun 1855   R. H. Andrews
                                       J. T. Roberts

Witnesses: N. A. Kidd, Webb Kidd
Recorded 21 Jun 1855

Book G, P 214
Know all men that I, John Bennett, have sold to George Lowery a negro man named Henry, 23, for $800.
13 Apr 1855   John Bennett
                                         George Lowery
Witnesses: George Thompson, W. C. Smith
Recorded 24 Apr 1855

Book G, P 216
Received of W. W. Bennett 10 bags of cotton and his note for 12 more bags to be delivered on or before March 1, 1856, for a negro girl named Cordelia and child, Malinda, 1. If same 22 bags of cotton not delivered by said date, the said W. W. Bennett agrees to pay me $1000, amount I paid for the slaves.
1 Mar 1855   William Thompson
                                         W. W. Bennett
Witnesses: John M. Thompson, William Henderson
Recorded 3 May 1855

Book G, P 219
Before me, William C. Smith, Parish Recorder, came Benjamin West, who declares he has sold to V. I. Bird certain negro slaves, Maria, 40, and Margaret (no age shown) and son Jerry, 4 months, for sum of $1650.
15 May 1855   Benjamin B. West
                                         V. I. Bird
Witnesses: James D. Griffin, John Nichols
Recorded 18 May 1855

Book G, P 227
Be it remembered that before me, William C. Smith, Parish Recorder, appeared Sylvanus Shepherd, who declares he has sold to V. I. Bird a negro woman named Matilda, 18, and child, Mariah, 10 months, for $1000.
2 Jun 1855   S. Shepherd
                                         V. I. Bird

Witnesses: Alex Shlenker, S. W. Ramsey
Recorded 4 Jun 1855

Book G, P 227
Before me, William C. Smith, Notary Public, came Valen I. Bird, who states he has sold to Simpson W. Ramsey, slaves acquired from John H. Wright, of Arkansas, for $900: Matilda, 18, and her daughter, Mariah, 10 months.

2 Jun 1855   V. I. Bird
                                  S. W. Ramsey
Witnesses: Alex Shlenker, S. Shepherd
Recorded 5 Jun 1855

Book G, P 249
Know all men that I, George Lowery, for the sum of $500, have sold a small negro boy named Major (No age shown.) to James Lowery.

28 Jul 1855   Geo Lowery
                                  James Lowery
Witnesses: (names obscure)
Recorded 20 Aug 1855

Book G, P 259
Know ye all men by these presents that I have sold to J. J. Loper a negro girl named Hester, 11, for $800.

5 Sep 1855   Elias George
                                  J. J. Loper
Witnesses: Dudley Grisham, W. L. George
Recorded 5 Sep 1855

Book G, P 280
In consideration of the sum of $750, I, Elizabeth Ann Green, wife of Solomon Powell, have sold to Samuel J. Larkin a negro slave named Rachel, 18.

12 Oct 1855   Elizabeth Ann Green
                                  Solomon Powell
                                  Samuel J. Larkin
Witnesses: J. R. Larkin, Daniel J. Tucker
Recorded 17 Oct 1855

115

Book G, P 281
Be it known that we, Joseph Stinson and wife Mary Stinson, of Jefferson Parish, have sold to L. Brunner of Union Parish a slave girl named Pherese (also spelled Ferese), 12, for $750.
5 May 1855   Joseph Stinson
                                           Mary Stinson
                                           L. Brunner
Witnesses: W. A. Andrews, Charles Mears
Recorded 28 Oct 1855

Book G, P 286
Received of William Thompson $1000 as payment for Cordelia, 18, and her daughter, Malinda, 2, negro slaves.
15 Oct 1855   W. W. Bennett
                                           William Thompson
Witness: John J. Bennett
Recorded 1 Nov 1855

Book G, P 304
Know all men that I have sold to Liberty K. Thomas a slave man named Abram for $1100.
26 Nov 1855   H. Regenburg
                                           Liberty K. Thomas
Witnesses: H. C. Glasson, H. B. Essick
Recorded 30 Nov 1855

Book G, P 308
Know ye all men by these presents that I, Flora Ann Skains, have sold to Uriel R. Milner, for the sum of $750, a negro boy named Amos, 6, and a negro girl, 9 months old. (No name shown.)
3 Dec 1855   Flora Ann Skains (her mark: X)
                                           U. R. Milner
Witnesses: W. T. Davis, M. J. Raney
Recorded 11 Dec 1855

Book G, P 310
Know ye all men by these presents that I have sold to John Edwards a negro slave named Andy, 28, for the sum of $800.
12 Dec 1855   F. M. Norman

John Edwards
Witnesses: C. L. Norman, Hansford Dean
Recorded 12 Dec 1855

Book G, P 311
Know ye all men by these presents that I, Hansford Dean, have sold to
John Edwards for the sum of $1200, a negro slave named Andy, 30.
7 Dec 1855   Hansford Dean
                                     John Edwards
Witnesses: H. B. Watters, G. Parsons
Recorded 12 Dec 1855

Book G, P 312
Be it remembered that I, John Edwards, have sold to J. M. Turner a
slave named Andy, 28, for $900.
13 Dec 1855   John Edwards
                                     J. M. Turner
Witnesses: H. B. Watters, James Edwards
Recorded 13 Dec 1855

Book G, P 314
Before me, William C. Smith, Parish Recorder, appeared Elijah W.
Miller, who states he has sold to John A. Bayless a negro slave named
Caroline, 34, for the sum of $600.
14 Dec 1855   Elijah W. Miller
                                     Jno. A. Bayless
Witnesses: M. S. Carson, Thomas C. Lewis
Recorded 14 Dec 1855

Book H, P 4
Before me, W. C. Smith, Parish Recorder, came V. I. Bird, who states
he has sold to Solomon Feazel a slave girl, Margaret, 18, and her son,
Jerry, 15 months, for $1200.
7 Jan 1856   V. I. Bird
                                     Solomon Feazel
Witnesses: John S. Barrett, S. O. Larche
Recorded 9 Jan 1856

Book H, P 11

Pursuant to an order of the 12th Judicial Court, I, William C. Smith, administrator of the estate of Samuel Montgomery, deceased, have sold slave property of the estate as follows. To George R. Murphey, a man named Hirome, 20, for $1305.
17 Jan 1856   William C. Smith
Witness: F. Haile
Recorded 17 Jan 1856

Book H, P 13
Received of Richard B. Williams $800 in payment for a slave girl, Elizabeth, 23.
17 Oct 1855   Jesse Tubb
                                         Richard B. Williams
Witnesses: William Edmond, James Patton
Recorded 17 Oct 1855

Book H, P 15
Pursuant to an order by the 12th Judicial Court, I, George Everett, administrator of the estate of Mary P. Ward, deceased, have sold to highest bidders, to pay debts, negro slave property as follows. To A. M. Johnson, for $1350, Winney, 15 and her infant; to W. D. M. Bruton, for $1200, Isaac, 38.
2 Jan 1856   George Everett
Witnesses: Samuel L. Robinson, James G. Gathright
Recorded 19 Jan 1856

Book H, P 22
Know all men that we have sold to Silvanus Sheppard for the sum of $1300, a slave girl named Jane, 19.
18 Jan 1856   F. H. Carr
                                         Allen Carr
                                         S. Sheppard
Witnesses: M. Steel Carson, M. B. H. Poor
Recorded 28 Jan 1856

Book H, P 28
Pursuant to an order of the 12th Judicial Court, I, Cullen Edwards, administrator of the estate of Thomas M. Hand, deceased, have sold to highest bidders at public auction the following negro slaves: To

Robertson Richardson, Easter, 27, for $1075. To Fergurson Haile, Willis, 23, for $1360. To Elijah Miller, Anthony, 35, for $1200. To H. C. Glasson, Ned, 35, for $692.
31 Jan 1856   Cullen Edwards, Exec
Witnesses: John L. Barrett, S. O. Larch
Recorded 1 Feb 1856

Book H, P 38
Pursuant to an order of the 12th Judicial Court, I, Daniel Sawyer, administrator of the estate of Willis Sawyer, deceased, have sold at auction negro slaves, to wit, to Daniel Sawyer, Liddy, 40, for $556, to James J. Sawyer, Matilda, 15, for $900, and to H. Davis Goyne, Allen, 12, for $900.
16 Feb 1856   Daniel Sawyer
Witnesses: Hiram Cooper (his mark: X), H. B. Essick
Recorded 26 Feb 1856

Book H, P 53
Received of A. E. Plyant payment for slaves as named. Ann, Eliza, Taylor, Jane, Winny and Governor. (No value or ages shown.)
29 Feb 1856   Elizabeth Stewart
                                     A. E. Plyant
Witnesses: John A. Hammock, Calvin Presley
Recorded 21 Oct 1857

Book H, P 56
Know all men by these presents that I have sold to Ann Kelley negro slaves, to wit, Squier, 24, Cindy, 11, Robert, 8, and Clow, a woman, 50, for total sum of $2500.
2 Aug 1855   John Kelley
                                     Ann Kelley
Witnesses: J. A. Creath, W. C. Smith
Recorded 24 Mar 1856

Book H, P 63
Pursuant to an order of the 12th Judicial Court, I sold to John Taylor a slave man named Joe, 20, for the sum of $1435, property of the estate of Calvin Y. Norman, deceased.
3 Apr 1856   Martha A. Edwards Norman,

wife of C. Y. Norman
Witness: J. C. Mayes
Recorded 3 Apr 1856

Book H, P 69
Know all men that I have sold to John Williams a slave girl named
Rose, 18, for $800.
2 Oct 1855   Israel B. Williams
                                     John Williams
Witnesses: John W. Hester, Thomas Simpson
Recorded 15 Apr 1856

Book H, P 79
Know all men by these presents that I have sold to John T. Matthews
the boy, Allen, 3, for $225.
16 Dec 1855   John O. Matthews
                                     John T. Matthews
Witnesses: S. T. Hayes, (second name obscure)
Recorded 21 Apr 1856

Book H, P 84
Know all men that I have sold to Thomas N. Skains, 2 slaves, Susan,
6, and Lewis, 3, for $1375.
29 Mar 1856   Flora Ann Skains (her mark: X)
                                     Thomas N. Skains
Witnesses: J. C. Mayes, E. G. Calk
Recorded 22 Apr 1856

Book H, P 85
Know all men that for the sum of $800, I have sold to Willis Wood, of
Jackson Parish, a slave boy, Jack, 15.
22 Apr 1856   Sarah Ann Raley
                                     Willis Wood
Witnesses: W. McFarland, E. M. Graham
Recorded 22 Apr 1856

Book H, P 87
Know ye that I, Thomas Ivey, have sold to John W. Thomas a negro
slave named Mary, 13, for $800.

22 Apr 1856   Thomas D. Ivey
                                               J. W. Thomas
Witnesses: S. O. Larche, H. B. Essick
Recorded 26 Apr 1856

Book H, P 90
Know all ye men by these presents that for the sum of $1500, I have
sold to Solomon Feazel a slave woman named Martha, 16, and her
children, Noah, 2, and Charity, 2 months.
28 Mar 1856   Benjamin F. Farmer
                                               Solomon Feazel
Witnesses: Susan Harris, T. J. Wilhite
Recorded 28 Mar 1856

Book H, P 107
In consideration of the affection I have for my daughter, Elizabeth N.
West, I give to her a slave girl named Emaly, 19.
24 Jun 1856   James E. Jones
                                               Lizzie N. West
Witness: Alex Shlenker
Recorded 26 Jun 1856

Book H, P 108
Pursuant to an order of the 12th Judicial Court, I, A. M. Callaway,
Sheriff, have sold to highest bidder a slave of the estate of B. B. West,
deceased, to James E. Jones the woman Emily, 19, for $300.
9 Jun 1856   A. M.Callaway
Witness: Wm C. Smith, Recorder
Recorded 26 Jun 1856

Book H, P 115
Pursuant to an order of the 12th Judicial Court, I have conducted a
sheriff's sale, and state that Elizabeth Brantley, former owner of a
negro slave, Henry (no age shown) sold said slave to Uriah Bass for
$1200.
8 Jul 1856   A. M. Callaway, Sheriff
Witnesses: S. O. Larche, A. A. Carr
Recorded 9 Jul 1856

121

Book H, P 116
By an order of the 12th Judicial Court, I, administrator of the estate of John Rogers, deceased, have sold to Wm Darby the following slaves, for the sum of $1175: Caroline, 18, and her daughters, Julian Ann, 3, and Jane, 10 months old.
8 Jul 1856   A. M. Callaway, Sheriff
                                             Wm. A. Darby
Witness: S. O. Larch
Recorded 9 Jul 1856

Book H, P 134
Before me, William C. Smith, Parish Recorder, came Solomon Feazel, who states he sold to V. I. Bird, the slaves Joshua, 47, and Lucinda, 35, for $1650.
21 Aug 1856   Solomon Feazel
                                             V. I. Bird
Witnesses: W. A. Darby, John L. Barrett
Recorded 25 Aug 1856

Book H, P 135
Received of Solomon Feazel the sum of $800 to pay for a slave named Bill, 12.
21 Aug 1856   V. I. Bird
                                             Solomon Feazel
Witnesses: W. A. Darby, J. S. Barrett
Recorded 26 Aug 1856

Book H, P 139
Know all men that I have sold to J. J. Loper for the sum of $1600 a slave girl named Rhoda, 15, and a boy named Joseph, 3.
25 Mar 1856   Miles W. Goldsby
                                             J. J. Loper
Witnesses: Elias George, W. C. Smith
Recorded 6 Sep 1856

Book H, P 172
Received of William R. Johnson the sum of $250 for a negro man named Peter, about 80 years old.
27 Oct 1856   H. C. Glasson

William R. Johnson

Witness: Thos Van Hook
Recorded 10 Nov 1856

Book H, P 182
Know ye all men that I, Charles Thompson, have purchased from T.
M. Smith certain slaves, for the sum of $5500: Joe, 42, and his wife,
Nicey, 24; Wesley, 24; Little Joe, 21, and his wife, Matilda, 16.
8 Nov 1856   T. M. Smith
                                        Charles J. Thompson
Witnesses: O. B. Hill, John V. Arrington
Recorded 17 Nov 1856

Book H, P 185
Know all men that I have sold to John T. Roberts, for $4200, slaves,
to wit, Booker, 38, Louisa, 40, Alexander, 12, Ralph, 10, Milley, 7,
Catherine, 5, Joe, 4, and Solomon, 1.
13 Dec 1855   James F. Roberts
                                        John T. Roberts
Witness: Thomas Brantley
Recorded 29 Nov 1856

Book H, P 198
Before me, William C. Smith, Parish Recorder, came Nancy Lowery,
wife of William W. Bennett, heirs of George Lowery, deceased, who
state they have sold to Ruffin Goldston Pleasant, slaves of the estate,
namely, Dick, 28, Pleasant, 36, and Jane, 12, for the sum of $4000.
20 Dec 1856   Nancy Bennett (her mark: X)   ·
                                        R. G. Pleasant
Witnesses: D. W. Fuller, Reuben Cole
Recorded 22 Dec 1856

Book H, P 225
Pursuant to an order of the 12th Judicial Court to partition the estate
of William A. Clark, deceased, I, Samuel Payne, with other legal
experts, Wm. H. Carson and Wm. C. Smith, have sold at auction the
following negro slaves to highest bidders as shown. Lot #1, Bob, 21,
to Sarah Bailey, for $1300. Lot #2, Hal, to Ellen Dillard, for $1300.

Lot #3, Bill, to Charles Clark for $800. Lot #4, Sophia, to Susan Clark for $800 (ages of slaves in Lots #2, #3 and #4 not shown).
4 Jan 1857   Samuel Payne
Witnesses: H. B. Essick, Henry Regenburg
Recorded 4 Jan 1857

Book H, P 228
Know all men by these presents that we, U. R. Milner and Mary Milner, have sold to James G. Kolb a negro girl named Laura, 14, for the sum of $1000.
9 Jan 1857   U. R. Milner
                                              Mary Milner
                                              James G. Kolb
Witnesses: Felix Hines, Jesse Glaze
Recorded 9 Jan 1857

Book H, P 248
Before me, W. C. Smith, Parish Recorder, came Lazarus and Emanuel Brunner who state they sold to V. I. Bird a slave girl, Penny, 50, for $400.
27 Jan 1857   Lazarus Brunner
                                              Emanuel Brunner
Witness: W. A. McFarland
Recorded 29 Jan 1857

Book H, P 252
In consideration of the sum of $9900, I have sold to W. L. Spears, certain negro slaves, viz. Peter, 60, his wife, Amy, 42, and their child, Cinderella, 9; John, 24, and his wife Chana, 20, and her children, Susan, 15, Eliza Jane, 2, and John Frederick, 4 weeks; Terry, 18, Jack, 16, Mitchell, 21, Lizetta, 14, and Henrietta, 12.
31 Oct 1856   Thomas Smith
                                              W. L. Spears
Witnesses: O. B. Hill, Azaniah Gillcoate
Recorded 3 Feb 1857

Book H, P 255

Know ye all men that I, William B. Mattox, have sold to Benjamin F. Farmer a negro boy, 12, for the sum of $100 (name of slave not shown).

7 Feb 1857   William B. Mattox
                               Benjamin F. Farmer
Witness: Solomon Feazel
Recorded 7 Feb 1857

Book H, P 261
Before me, William C. Smith, Parish Recorder, came S. H. Perry, who states he has sold to J. A. Bayless two slaves, Salina, 10, and Harriett, 18, for $2100.

6 Feb 1857   S. H. Perry
                               J. A. Bayless
Witness: A. H. Granger
Recorded 14 Feb 1857

Book H, P 262
Before me, William C. Smith, Parish Recorder, came John A. Bayless, who states that for the sum of $1500 he has sold to Samuel H. Perry a slave man named Joseph, 18.

14 Feb 1857   J. A. Bayless
                             S. H. Perry
Witnesses: A. K. Grayson, W. A. Glasson
Recorded 14 Feb 1857

Book H, P 270
Received of Martha Jane Cooper, Wife of Hynson Cooper, the sum of $1150, in payment for a negro slave named Jim, 37.

27 Jan 1857   Mary Jane Calvert
                             Mary Jane Cooper
Witnesses: John Boatwright, B. F. Ratcliff
Recorded 11 Mar 1857

Book H, P 282
Know all men that I, Horatio McLaine, of Jackson Parish, have sold to James E. Jones of Winn Parish, a negro slave boy named Sam, 14, for $1500.

25 Jan 1857   Horatio McLaine

James E. Jones
Witnesses: W. A. Glasson, L. Brunner
Recorded 27 Mar 1857

Book H, P 283
Know ye all men that I, James E. Jones, have sold to Benjamin B. West a slave man, Shadrick, 22, for $1200.
28 Mar 1857   · J. E. Jones
                                           B. B. West
Witnesses: II. D. Essick, II. Regenberg
Recorded 28 Mar 1857

Book H, P 284
Be it known that I, G. W. Reed, a resident of Scott County, Arkansas, have sold to James E. Jones, of Winn Parish, a negro named Monroe, 22, for $1050.
1 Jan 1857   G. W. Reed
                                 J. E. Jones
Witnesses: Allen Carr, L. Brunner
Recorded 28 Mar 1857

Book H, P 285
Know ye all men that I, Benjamin M. McClelland, have sold to Joel Smith, a negro girl, 22, named Tennessee, for $1000.
1 Oct 1856   Benjamin McClelland
                                 Joel Smith
Witnesses: Frederick M. McClelland, Joseph A. Wickliff
Recorded 1 Apr 1857

Book H, P 285
Know ye that I, Lewis Brown, of Clay County in Mississippi, in consideration of the sum of $1900, have sold to J. E. Jones, of Winn Parish, two slave girls, Clara, 16, and Elvira, 14.
27 Mar 1857   Lewis Brown
                                 J. E. Jones
Witnesses: John A. Bayless, S. W. Ramsey
Recorded 27 Mar 1857

Book H, P 286

Know all men that I, Benjamin McClelland, have sold to Joel Smith a negro woman named Emily, 22, and her child, David, for $1200. (No age shown.)

1 Oct 1856   Benjamin McClelland
                               Joel Smith

Witnesses: Joseph A. Wickliff, Frederick M. McClelland
Recorded 1 Apr 1857

Book H, P 299
Know ye all men by these presents that, for the sum of $1050, I have sold to L. Brunner a negro slave named Ann, 20.

30 Mar 1857   Alex Shlenker
                               L. Brunner

Witnesses: David Arent, Henry March
Recorded 9 Apr 1857

Book H, P 303
Received of Alexander M. Taylor the sum of $800 in payment for a slave girl named Sharlett, 14.

8 Apr 1857   James A. Taylor
                               Alexander M. Taylor

Witness: John H. Taylor
Recorded 20 Apr 1857

Book H, P 307
Before me, Wm C. Smith, Parish Recorder, came W. H. Sloane, who declares that for $2800, he sold to Daniel Payne, 2 slaves, Jock, 21, and Hanah, 19.

15 Apr 1857   William Slone
                               Daniel Payne

Witnesses: S. O. Larche, Charles Beck
Recorded 20 Apr 1857

Book H, P 311
Received of R. G. Pleasant the sum of $1350, payment for a slave man named Mitchell, 21.

3 Jan 1857   W. L. Spears
                               R. G. Pleasant

Witnesses: A. J. Hunt, Jeremiah Hayes

Recorded 21 Apr 1857

Book H, P 315
Know all men that we, W. D. M. Bruton and Nancy Bruton, have sold to Jane A. McFadin, for $1000, a negro girl named Matilda, 12.

23 Apr 1857	W. D. M. Bruton
	Nancy Bruton
	Jane A. McFadin

Witnesses: John P. Everett, R. H. Andrews
Recorded 23 Apr 1857

Book H, P 317
Received of Frances McClelland the sum of $845, in payment for a negro slave girl named Rachiel, 10.

| 26 Feb 1857 | James Lowery |
| | Frances McClelland |

Witnesses: N. M. Patton, F. C. McClelland
Recorded 27 Apr 1857

Book H, P 320
In consideration of the sum of $2600, I have sold to V. I. Bird four slaves, Harriett, 32, Angeline, 7, Nicy, 5, and Willis, 2.

| 17 Apr 1857 | W. H. Coker |
| | V. I. Bird |

Witnesses: Henry March, Jacob Shlenker
Recorded 28 Apr 1857

Book H, P 322
By order of the 12th Judicial Court, I, Mary C. Ellis, administrator of the estate of Reuben Ellis, deceased, have sold following slaves to highest bidders. To W. A. Glasson, Mose, 33, for $1495. To Hiram Peavy, Matt, 13, for $950. To Mary C. Ellis, Martha, 56, for $700. To M. B. Lee, Mariah, 36, for $492.

7 Feb 1857   Mary C. Ellis
Witnesses: G. Brunner, S. O. Larch
Recorded 30 Apr 1857

Book H, P 331

Before me, William C. Smith, Parish Recorder, appeared Britten Honeycuttt, who swears he has sold to Robert Matthews a negro girl named Susan, 13, for the sum of $100.

12 May 1857   Britten Honeycutt
                                                       Robert Matthews

Witnesses: T. W. Findley, William H. Carson
Recorded 12 May 1857

Book H, P 332
Know ye all men that I, Henry Regenburg, have sold the following slaves to J. B. Ivey, for total sum of $1500: Peggy, 35, and children, Legrand, 7, Nice, 5, Herrard, 3, and Sally, 1.

5 May 1857   Henry Regenburg
                                                       J. B. Ivey

Witnesses: J. G. Hollis, Wm C. Smith
Recorded 13 May 1857

Book H, P 334
Know ye all men that in consideration of the sum of $3800, I, Elizabeth Lowery, have sold to Larkin Lowery 4 slaves, viz, Winney, 55, Andy, 30, Hannah, 25, and Diana, 17.

21 May 1857   Elizabeth Lowery (her mark: X)
                                                       Larkin Lowery

Witnesses: Henry W. Harper, H. Regenburg
Recorded 29 May 1857

Book H, P 344
By virtue of an order of the 12th Judicial Court, I, A. M. Callaway, Sheriff, have sold to John R. Aulds the following slaves: Charity, 22, and her children, Henry, 6, and Frances, 3, for the sum of $2100.

30 Jun 1857   A. M. Callaway
                                                       John R. Aulds

Witnesses: David Ward, James A. Aulds
Recorded 30 Jun 1857

Book H, P 352
Be it remembered that before me, William C. Smith, Parish Recorder, appeared David M. Jameson who declares he sold a negro slave named Lemuel, 23, to George Feazel, for the sum of $1500.

30 Jul 1857   David M. Jameson
                                      George Feazel
Witnesses: S. O. Larche, S. Feazel
Recorded 31 Jul 1857

Book H, P 353
Know ye men that I, E. M. Aulds, have sold to John E. Green a negro
slave named Albert, 43, for $1200.
8 Jun 1857   Elijah Michael Aulds
                                      John Ernal Green
Witnesses: J. T. B. Andrews, Shadrick Johnson
Recorded 31 Jul 1857

Book H, P 357
In consideration of the love I have for my daughter, Narcissa Elizabeth
Williams, wife of Israel B. Williams, I give to her a slave girl named
Rose, 20.
7 Jul 1857   James Morris (his mark: X)
                                      Narcissa Eliza Williams
Witnesses: Anderson Lee, William Dearing (Deed was executed in
Barbour County, Alabama, recorded in Union Parish 3 Aug 1857.)

Book H, P 357
Know ye all men that I, John P. Everett, have sold to Thomas M.
McFadin, for the sum of $1350, a negro boy, named Gillis, 15.
3 Aug 1857   John P. Everett
                                      Thomas M. McFadin
Witness: John Dennis
Recorded 3 Aug 1857

Book H, P 373
Know ye that I have sold to Davis Rayburn a negro woman named
Silla, 38, for $750.
16 Apr 1857   Reuben D. Black
                                      David Rayburn
Witnesses: O. B. Hill, George M. Morgan
Recorded 11 Sep 1857

Book H, P 408

Know all men that I have given to Amanda Elizabeth Plyant, wife of Henry Plyant, slaves, to wit, Sarah, 39, Rufus, 18, Eliza, 13, Taylor, 12, Jane, 10, Winney, 8, and Governor, 5.

19 Oct 1857   George D. Stewart
                               A. E. Plyant

Witnesses: names obscure
Recorded 20 Oct 1857

Book H, P 413
Know ye that I have sold to Mary Ann Mixon, a resident of Ashley County, Arkansas, a slave girl named Minty, 11, for $600.

26 Oct 1857   James E. Jones
                               Mary Ann Mixon

Witnesses: David Arent, L. Brunner
Recorded 26 Oct 1857

Book H, P 439
Before me, W. C. Smith, came E. A. Rossiter, who says she has sold to V. I. Bird a slave girl, Delilah, 16, for $1000.

14 Dec 1857   Eliza Ann Rossiter
                               V. I. Bird

Witnesses: J. W. Ramsey, James A. Douglass
Recorded 16 Dec 1856

Book H, P 442
Received of E. B. Windes the sum of $2400, payment for two negro slaves, Andrew, 35, and Emilaine, 16.

10 Mar 1858   Allen Carr
                               E. B. Windes

Witnesses: W. A. Darby, Thomas Van Hook
Recorded 21 Dec 1858

Book H, P 443
Know ye all men that I have sold to J. T. Morrison a slave named George, 8, for $700.

23 Dec 1857   Nancy Maledy
                               J. T. Morrison

Witnesses: J. A. Kidd, W. H. Brown (his mark: X)
Recorded 23 Dec 1857

Book H, P 448
Before me, William C. Smith, Parish Recorder, appeared Samuel Smith, who declares he has sold to John Smith for $1500, a negro man named Gabriel, 35, a negro girl named Charlotte, 18, and her infant, Maria.
4 Jan 1858   Samuel Smith
                                             John Smith
Witnesses: William C. Parker, E. A. Reppond
Recorded 4 Jan 1858

Book H, P 450
Be it known that we have sold to J. E. Jones a slave girl named Quint, 8, for $475.
6 Jan 1858   John Grey
                                             Sarah Grey
                                             J. E. Jones
Witnesses: F. L. Brown, Riley Agerton
Recorded 6 Jan 1858

Book H, P 454
Know all men that I, John A. Dixon, have sold to William White a slave of the estate of Mixon D. Dixon, deceased, for $1003, a girl named Martha, 22.
6 Jan 1858   John A. Dixon
                                             William White
Witnesses: Robert J. Caldwell, John L. Barrett
Recorded 6 Jan 1858

Book H, P 461
Know ye all men that I have sold to Joseph Baker a slave named Mose, 22, for $1000.
28 Dec 1858   J. G. Taylor
                                             Joseph Baker
Witnesses: E. B. Windes, F. H. Carr
Recorded 13 Jan 1859

Book H, P 463

Know ye all men that I, Joseph Baker, have sold to Jordan G. Taylor a slave boy named Madison, 17. (No value shown.)

28 Dec 1857	Joseph Baker
	Jordan G. Taylor

Witnesses: E. B. Windes, F. H. Carr
Recorded 18 Jun 1858

Book H, P 468
Know ye all men that we, Mary A. Bryant, James R. Bryant, Sallie H. Rowland, Virginia C. Terrell, W. S. Terrell, L. F. Rowland, grantors, have sold to Alexander Shlenker, a negro boy named Shaddeus, 12, for $1000.

18 Jan 1858	Mary A. Bryant
	Alexander Shlenker

Witnesses: G. Mayes, A. H. Granger
Recorded 18 Jan 1858

Book H, P 484
Know all ye men by these presents that I, V. I. Bird, have sold to Mary C. Ellis a slave girl named Delilah, 16, for the sum of $1200.

30 Jan 1858	V. I. Bird
	Mary C. Ellis

Witnesses: Henry March, S. O. Larch
Recorded 3 Feb 1858

Book H, P 505
In consideration of the sum of $1150, I have sold to V. I. Bird a negro boy, Sandford, 12, for $1150.

19 Feb 1858	Wm. A. Glasson
	V. I. Bird

Witnesses: W. H. Carson, M. S. Carson
Recorded 23 Feb 1858

Book H, P 506
Know all men that I have sold to William Rabun certain negro slaves, for $2300. Eveline, 20, and her children, Catherine, 5, Elias, 2, and Jackson, infant.

23 Feb 1858	Susan Davis (her mark: X),
	wife of William R. Davis

Wm. Rabun
Witnesses: W. J. Goyne, G. T. Dickenson
Recorded 25 Feb 1858

Book H, P 514
Let it be known that we have sold to A. Bearden a slave girl, Eliza, 18,
for $1217.
3 Mar 1858   Brunner and Brother
                                        Arthur Bearden (his mark: X)
Witnesses: William Pipes, David Arent
Recorded 6 Mar 1858

Book H, P 515
Know ye all men by these presents that we, Brunner & Brother, have
sold to William Pipes a slave man, Daniel, 27, for $1450.
5 Mar 1858   Brunner & Brother
                                        Wm. Pipes
Witnesses: John E. Green, David Arent
Recorded 6 Mar 1858

Book H, P 516
Know ye all men that we, Brunner and Brother, have sold to E. D.
Sled a negro man named George, 22, for $1450.
1 Mar 1858   Brunner and Brother
                                        E. D. Sled
Witnesses: F. H. Carr, David Arent
Recorded 6 May 1858

Book H, P 538
Know ye all men that I, T. E. Matthews, have sold to Lewis M. Powell
3 slaves, Richard, 20, Edward, 18, and Henry Waters, for $4200.
10 Feb 1857   Thomas E. Matthews
                                        Lewis M. Powell
Witnesses: Samuel G. Ferguson, C. T. Powell
Recorded 10 Feb 1857

Book H, P 540

In consideration of the sum of $900, I, George W. Robinson, of Jackson County, Florida, have sold to John J. Loper a negro boy named Augustus, 15, for $900.

20 Mar 1858   George W. Robinson
                                           John J. Loper
Witnesses: Elias George, T. M. Foster
Recorded 23 Mar 1858

Book H, P 541
Be it known that I, James M. Foster, of Indianola, Texas, have sold to Louisa Loper a negro girl named Sarah Ann, 13, for $900.

23 Mar 1858   James M. Foster
                                           Louisa Loper
Witnesses: Elias George, S. W. Ramsey
Recorded 23 Mar 1858

Book H, P 542
Know all men by these presents that we, Levi and Meyer, have sold to John J. Loper a negro man named Ned, 28, for $1300.

20 Mar 1858   M. Levi
                                           G. Meyer
                                           John J. Loper
Witnesses: G. N. Benson, Elias George
Recorded 23 Mar 1858

Book I, P 1
Before me, William C. Smith, Parish Recorder, appeared J. E. Prestidge who declares he has sold to J. J. Loper a negro slave named Dick, 26, for $1200.

10 Mar 1858   J. E. Prestidge
                                           J. J. Loper

Witness: A. P. Johnson
(Deed was executed in Selma, Alabama, recorded in Union Parish 12 Apr 1858)

Book I, P 11

Know ye all men that I, L. C. Callaway, have sold to John B. Robertson, 2 negro slaves, Anne, 18, and Tom, 17, for the sum of $2600.
15 Apr 1858   L. C. Callaway
                                     John B. Robertson
Witnesses: A. M. Callaway, W. W. Guthrie
Recorded 20 Apr 1858

Book I, P 19
Received of John H. Patterson the sum of $300 in payment for a slave girl named Melissa, 10.
25 Dec 1857   Argus Patterson
                                     John H. Patterson
Witness: Robert G. Taylor
Recorded 10 May 1858

Book I, P 23
Pursuant to an order of the 12th Judicial Court, I, William C. Smith, administrator of the estate of Peter Lankford, deceased, sold slaves of the estate, to wit, to Allen M. Callaway for $1255, Joe, 22. To Henry Regenburg for $1285, Green, 20. To William A. Parks for $975, Mariah, 14.
3 Apr 1858   William C. Smith
Witnesses: H. Regenburg, H. B. Essick
Recorded 12 May 1858

Book I, P 24
Pursuant to an order by the 12th Judicial Court, I, William C. Smith, Parish Recorder and Notary Public, have sold at auction, negro slaves of the estate of Peter Lankford, deceased, to wit, Ceasor, 18, for $910, and Allick, 16, for $935 (Ceasor to V. I. Bird and Allick to Henry Regenburg).
12 May 1858   Wm C. Smith, administrator
Witnesses: John McCaskey, H. B. Essick
Recorded 12 May 1858

Book I, P 41
Know all men that I have sold to Thomas J. Stewart a slave boy named Shaddeuz, 12, for $1000.

11 Jun 1858   Alexander Shlenker
                                     Thomas J. Stewart
Witnesses: Savory O. Larche, Henry March
Recorded 23 Jun 1858

Book I, P 49
In consideration of the sum of $1165, I have sold to D. G. Ferguson 2
negro slaves, Reddico, a man, 38, and Nancy, 16.
3 Dec 1857   Abram Hutchinson
                                     D. G. Fergusan
Witnesses: John B. Callahan, E. H. Ferguson (Deed was executed in
Butler County, Alabama, recorded in Union Parish 9 Jul 1858)

Book I, P 53
Know ye all men by these presents that we, S. David Mims and Mary
W. Mims, man and wife, have sold a slave named Ned, 28, to the firm
of Levi and Meyer, for the sum of $1300.
10 Jul 1858   S. D. Mims
                                     M. W. Mims
                                     Max Levi
                                     Gabriel Meyer
Witnesses: Wm. E. Ross, James Ross
Recorded 10 Dec 1858

Book I, P 54
I, Ellen McClelland, declare I have sold to Joel Smith, 4 slaves, viz,
Emily, 23, and her children, David, 3, and Joanna, 7 months, for
$1550; and a girl, Tennessee, 24, for $1100.
14 Mar 1858   Ellen McClelland
                                     Joel Smith
Witnesses: James W. Howe, F. G. Hargis
Recorded 12 Jul 1858

Book I, P 66
Received of Mary Culverhouse the sum of $500 in payment for 1
negro slave girl named Ann, 18.
16 Dec 1845   Thomas M. Hand
                                     Mary Culverhouse
Witnesses: John Calderwood, W. M. Lawrence

137

Recorded 28 Jul 1846

Book I, P 80
By common consent, the heirs of John Bennett, deceased, agreed to partition said estate amicably, setting apart slaves of the estate as follows: for Margaret Bennett, widow, Rufus, 15, and Clara, 50. For Nancy C. Bennett, Sam, 33. For William W. Bennett, York, 22, and Till, 40 and children, Haly/Harvey? and Edull (ages not shown). For Harriett B. Bennett, wife of Wm Thompson, Jane, 33, and children, Martha, 16, Sarah, Silver and Marion, all under 10. For Nancy C. Bennett (Smith), Olive, 22, and child, Charles, and Rudy, 16, and Willis, 15.

24 Sep 1858   Margaret Bennett (her mark: X)
Witnesses: H. Regenburg, John W. Henderson (his mark: X)
Recorded 24 Sep 1858

Book I, P 110
Know all men that I have sold to Samuel L. Wright a slave woman named Harriett, and her child, Willis, 3, for $1500.

26 Mar 1858   V. I. Bird
                                   S. L. Wright
Witnesses: M. Weil, C. M. Smith
Recorded 16 Mar 1858

Book I, P 124
Received of Elizabeth Tatum the sum of $900, payment for a negro girl named Juliann. (No age shown.)

18 May 1858   John Wright
                                   Elizabeth Tatum
Witnesses: J. G. Wright, D. M. Wright
Recorded 9 Nov 1858

Book I, P 158
Before me, William C. Smith, Parish Recorder, came Wiley Cook who declares that in consideration of the love he has for his daughter, Elizabeth Jane Cook, he has given her the following slaves: Dianah, 23, and her children, Hester, 4, George, 5, and Jack, 6 months; and a girl named Lucy, 14, with a total value of $1925.

10 Dec 1858   Wiley Cook

Elizabeth Jane Cook Moore,
wife of William C. Moore
Witnesses: George Little, J. J. Norris
Recorded 10 Dec 1858

Book I, P 197
Know ye all men that I have sold to E. B. Windes, for the sum of $1400, certain slaves, to wit, Tennessee, 60, her daughter, Sarah Ann, 32, and Sarah's son, 11 (name not shown).
30 Dec 1858   Allen Carr
                                     E. B. Windes
Witnesses: W. A. Darby, S. C. Lee
Recorded 5 Jan 1859

Book I, P 198
Know all men that I, Allen Carr, have sold to John Taylor certain slaves, to wit, Frank, 7, Dianna, 32, Jeff, 14, Green, 23, Mary, 9, Dicy, 11, and Arrina, 6. (No value shown.)
21 Mar 1858   Allen Carr
                                     John Taylor
Witnesses: George A. Killgore, E. B. Windes
Recorded 5 Jan 1859

Book I, P 212
Received of George A. Stinson the sum of $700, payment for a negro boy named Primus. (No age shown.)
17 Dec 1858   John Stow
                                     George A. Stinson
Witnesses: John B. Mitchell, F. E. McGee
Recorded 21 Jan 1859

Book I, P 229
Know ye men that I, David G. Temple, have sold to John L. Barrett certain negro slaves, viz, Molly, 24, and her children, Charlotte, 8, and Walter, 4, for the sum of $1800.
2 Feb 1859   D. G. Temple
                                     John L. Barrett
Witnesses: H. M. Barrett, Savory O. Larche
Recorded 2 Feb 1859

139

Book I, P 243
Know ye all men that in consideration of the sum of $1023, we have
sold to T. J. Gilbert a slave named Henry, 45.
22 Dec 1858   L. C. Thompson
                                     J. L. Thompson
                                     R. E. Thompson
                                     (Grantors)
                                     T. J. Gilbert (Grantee)
Witnesses: G. M. Morgan, D. M. Jameson
Recorded 7 Feb 1859

Book I, P 245
Know all men by these presents that I, John W. Thomas, for the sum
of $1500, have sold to H. G. Hollis, 2 negro slaves, Mary, 15, and
child, Louis, 18 months.
28 Oct 1858   John W. Thomas
                                     H. G. Hollis
Witnesses: J. B. Ivey, Nancy Edwards
Recorded 7 Feb 1859

Book I, P 270
Know all men that I have sold to J. T. Morrison a slave girl named
Caroline, 10, for $500.
11 Apr 1858   A. J. Matthews
                                     J. T. Morrison
Witnesses: F. B. Matthews, J. Telford
Recorded 15 Feb 1859

Book I, P 273
Before me, William C. Smith, Parish Recorder, came George W.
Reynolds, who decares that in consideration of the love and affection
he has for his daughter, Eily A. Reynolds, now wife of Francis
McCormick, and for her filial duty towards him, he has given to her a
negro slave girl named Mary, 11, valued at $900.
17 Feb 1859   George W. Reynolds
                                     Emily A. McCormick
Witnesses: T. Wilhite, J. B. Sanders
Recorded 19 Feb 1859

Book I, P 281
This indenture made between S. W. Phillips and M. Wiel, second party to pay to first party by January 1, 1861, the sum of $400 for a slave boy, named Sam, 22, or if not paid by that date, to deliver to first party, provisions, merchandise, and cotton, in lieu of cash payment.
12 May 1860   Silas W. Phillips
                                            M. Wiel
Witnesses: James M. Supo, N. W. Gunter
Recorded 23 Jun 1860

Book I, P 291
Know ye all men that I, Benjamin Smith, have sold to R. W. Windes for total of $7500, certain slaves, to wit, Ben, 30, Hanah, 22, and her children, Amanda, 6, James, Samuel, 2, Issy, infant; Mary, 24, and her children, Ruthy, 2, and Lucinda, 5 months; Rachel, 24, and her children, Anne, 2, and Austin, 5 months.
21 Feb 1859   Benjamin F. Smith
                                            R. W. Windes
Witnesses: W. A. Darby, E. M. Dean
Recorded 21 Feb 1859

Book I, P 295
Know ye that I, Alfred C. McKeen, in consideration of the sum of $2000, have sold to Francis M. McCormick, 4 slaves, to wit, Lizzie, 40, Columbus, 14, Emmett, 12, and Mary, 10.
20 Feb 1859   A. C. McKeen
                                            Francis McCormick
Witnesses: J. H. Flournoy, A. F. Flournoy
Recorded 24 Feb 1859

Book I, P 306
Know ye all men that I have sold to Thomas D. Ivey a negro boy named Legrand for $473. (No age shown.)
5 Jan 1859   Reuben Edwards
                                            Thomas D. Ivey
Witnesses: J. W. Scott, J. B. Ivey
Recorded 7 Mar 1859

Book I, P 311
Pursuant to an order of the 12th Judicial Court, I, A. M. Callaway, have sold to highest bidders at auction the following slaves, namely, Will, 18, to S. A. Doty, for $1870. Spencer, 30, to Joseph Baker, for $1550. Nathan, 40, to Britten Honeycutt, for $1310. Lucy and her children, Bird and Thomas (no ages shown) for $2015, to Hiram Cooper. Margaret, 24, to E. G. Bilberry, for $1320.
3 Feb 1859   A. M. Callaway, Sheriff
Witnesses: John L. Barrett, H. M. Barrett
Recorded 8 Mar 1859

Book I, P 315
Know ye all men that I have sold to John Taylor a slave girl named Sarah, 16, for $900.
12 Mar 1859   Sarah Dean
                                     John Taylor

Witnesses: S. C. Lee, W. A. Darby
Recorded 16 Mar 1859

Book I, P 317
In consideration of the sum of $1150, I, V. I. Bird, have sold to John M. Lee a negro boy named Sandford, 13.
5 Jan 1859   V. I. Bird
                                    John M. Lee
Witnesses: John Taylor, E. B. Windes
Recorded 16 Mar 1859

Book I, P 333
Know all men that we, H. J. Tignor and Anna Tignor, have sold to Etheldred Sled 2 slaves, Martha, 19, and infant, for the sum of $1400.
26 Feb 1859   H. J. Tignor
                                     Anna Tignor
                                     Etheldred Sled

Witnesses: O. B. Hill, T. J. Hollis
Recorded 8 Apr 1859

Book I, P 345
Before me, Benjamin D. Sheppard, Parish Recorder, came William B. Wallace and his wife Elizabeth, who declare they have sold to William

Oliver, certain slaves, to wit, Peter, 29, George, 12, Ellen, 10, Ned, 30, Horton, 12, Jefferson, 23, Elvira, 29, and her child, Ann, 18 months; Marshall, 6, Henry, 4, and Jim, 18. Value of slaves and land: $16,000.

1 Apr 1859   W. B. Wallace
                       Elizabeth Wallace
                       William Oliver

Witnesses: Hervey Drake, William A. Collins
Recorded 5 Apr 1859

Book I, P 351
Be it known that I, A. Smith, have sold to Liberty K. Thomas 2 slaves, James, 20, and Nancy, 15, for $2000.

15 Mar 1858   A. Smith
                       Liberty K. Thomas

Witnesses: John B. Womack, J. C. Wiggins (Deed was executed in Richmond, Virginia, recorded in Union Parish 13 Apr 1859.)

Book I, P 380
Know ye all men that I have sold to George Tubb the following slaves: Avery, 21, and Clarissy, 11, for $2000.

18 Apr 1859   Benj Tubb
                       Geo. Tubb

Witness: J. M. Johnson
Recorded 18 Apr 1859

Book I, P 384
Before me, William C. Smith, Parish Recorder, came G. A. Stinson, attorney for Berry Fuller, who states that on behalf of the said Fuller, he has sold to Elias Taylor negro slaves, viz, Matilda, 30, and her son, Enis, 7, for $1200.

23 Apr 1859   G. A. Stinson
                       Elias Taylor (his mark: X)

Witness: A. F. Crawford
Recorded 25 Apr 1859

Book I, P 424

Before me, William C. Smith, Parish Recorder, came Jesse Tubb, who states he has sold to George Tubb a slave man named Michel, 25, for $1700.

5 Jul 1859   Jesse Tubb
                                              George Tubb
Witnesses: John Holliday, J. B. Tubb
Recorded 5 Jul 1859

Book I, P 461
Know all men by these presents that we, R. K. Love and Emilette Ambleton Love, have sold to W. A. Glasson for the total sum of $5000, slaves, to wit, Matilda, 26, Caroline, 10, Peter, 15, Amanda, 14, Delilah, 13, Stephen, 9, and Phronia, 15, and her child, Bob. (No age shown.)

4 Aug 1859   R. K. Love
                                              Emilette Love (her mark: X)
Witnesses: F. G. Hargis, Jared Robinson
Recorded 8 Aug 1859

Book I, P 483
Know ye all men that I, Thomas McCormick, have sold to G. W. Sims a slave boy named Jim, 13, for $475.

17 Aug 1859   Thomas McCormick
                                              G. W. Sims
Witnesses: James B. Wilson, B. W. Futch
Recorded 31 Aug 1859

Book I, P 516
Know all men by these presents, that I, Royal K. Love and my wife Emilette Ambleton Love, in consideration of the sum of $5000, have sold to Alexander Ambleton, 4 negro slaves, Corissee, 10, Peter, 15, Dalilah, 13, and Stephen, 9.

24 Aug 1859   R. K. Love
                                              Emilette Love (her mark: X)
Witnesses: J. M. Turner, Jarred Robinson
Recorded 22 Sep 1859

Book I, P 519

Before me, William C. Smith, Parish Recorder, came Austin Martin, administrator of the estate of Joicy Martin, deceased, who declares he has sold to Thomas J. Martin a slave, Lewis, 25, property of the estate, for $1656.

25 Sep 1859   Austin Martin
                           Thomas J. Watson

Witnesses: D. C. Hicks, J. B. Sanders
Recorded 25 Sep 1859

Book I, P 523
In consideration of the sum of $3200, I, Benjamin F. Dillard, have sold to Thomas Mercer Smith, who resides in Natchitoches Parish, the following negro slaves. Betsy, 35, and her child, Nelly, 9, and Henry, a negro man, 21.

16 Sep 1859   Benjamin F. Dillard
                          Thomas M. Smith

Witnesses: H. H. Ham, Charles N. V. Clarke
Recorded 6 Oct 1859

Book I, P 530
Pursuant to an order of the 12th Judicial Court, I sold at auction to Francis McCormick, highest bidder of $1250 for a slave man named Charles, 36, property of the estate of Catherine M. McCormick, deceased.

21 Jun 1859   A. M. Callaway, Sheriff

Witnesses: William Cooper, W. Autry
Recorded 12 Oct 1859

Book I, P 534
Before me, Wm C. Smith, Parish Recorder, appeared George W. Sims who declared he sold to V. I. Bird a negro boy, 13, named Jim, for $600.

13 Oct 1859   G. W. Sims
                          V. I. Bird

Witnesses: John W. Scott, Joseph W. Terry
Recorded 13 Oct 1859

Book J, P 1

Before me, William C. Smith, Parish Recorder, appeared John G. Stocks, of the Parish of Ouachita, who declares that for $3500, he has sold to J. T. B. Andrews negro slaves, viz, Robert, 11, Henry, 11, George, 14, and Eliza, 6.
13 Oct 1859   John G. Stocks
                          J. T. B. Andrews
Witnesses: J. C. Manning, S. T. Wheelis
Recorded 13 Oct 1859

Book J, P 16
Know ye that I have sold to A. M. Taylor a negro slave named Jack, 50, for $800.
1 Oct 1859   John Matthews
                         A. M. Taylor
Witnesses: A. J. Matthews, David Futch
Recorded 11 Nov 1859

Book J, P 21
Before me, William C. Smith, Parish Recorder, came Wm. Fox, who declares he sold to James A. Aulds a negro woman slave named Maria, 37, for $700.
18 Nov 1859   Wm. Fox
                         James A. Aulds
Witnesses: Charles W. Lawrence, W. H. Carson
Recorded 18 Nov 1859

Book J, P 46
Know ye all men by these presents that I, James C. Manning, in consideration of the love and affection I have for my daughter, Elizabeth A. Manning, wife of William C. Smith, I give to her the negro woman, Matilda, 20, valued at $1100.
6 Dec 1859   James C. Manning
                         Elizabeth A. Smith
Witnesses: W. W. Guthrie, W. S. Callaway
Recorded 6 Dec 1859

Book J, P 48

In consideration of the love and affection I have for my son, George Little and his children (not named), I give to them negro slaves, to wit, Milly Ann, 20, and children, Walton, 5, and Camelia, 3.

12 Apr 1859   Catharine Little
                           George Little

Witnesses: Phillip Morris, Theopholus Johnson
(Deed was executed in Taliaferro County, Georgia, recorded in Union Parish 8 Dec 1859)

Book J, P 49
Know ye all men that I, W. D. Cooper, have sold to J. J. Loper for $4000, following slaves: Theo, 38, Mary, 27, Henry, 8, Caroline, 7, and Julie, 8 months.

10 Dec 1859   W. D. Cooper
                           J. J. Loper

Witnesses: T. L. Cooper, Dave Arent
Recorded 12 Dec 1859

Book J, P 62
Before me, William C. Smith, Parish Recorder, came James Hart of Memphis in the State of Tennessee, who declares that in consideration of affection he has for Louisa C. Loche, wife of James R. Ross of Union Parish, he being her brother-in-law and former tutor, he has this day donated to her the following property, to wit, Emanuel, 21, worth $1300, Simon, 27, worth $1300. Adam, 30, worth $1200, Phillis, 17, and her infant child, worth $1220, Lucy, 30, and her children, George, 7, Marsella, 5, and an infant, worth $2000. Shilla, 14, worth $1400, Louisa, 40, worth $500, Anderson, 22, worth $1500, Ike, 17, worth $1500, Becca, 30, worth $600, Wash, 40, worth $1200, Hagar, a woman, 50, worth $200, Millie, 17, and her child Mary, 1, worth $1000, and Aley, 17, and her infant, worth $1000, all together estimated at the sum of $17,000.

17 Dec 1859   James Hart
                        James R. Ross

Witnesses: S. David Mims, Robert L. Mims
Recorded 19 Dec 1859 (Reference Book J, P 61, James R. Ross had sold to James Hart, on 17 Dec 1859, recorded 19 Dec 1859, all of the slave indicated above, same witnesses.)

Book J, P 67
Before me, William C. Smith, Parish Recorder, came James G. Kolb, who states that he has sold to James A. Manning the slave woman Laura, 17, and child, 3 months old, for the sum of $1300.
26 Dec 1859   James G. Kolb
                               James A. Manning
Witnesses: James C. Manning, Heremiah G. Hicks
Recorded 26 Dec 1859

Book J, P 71
Know ye all men that I, Jacob Shlenker, have sold to J. J. Loper a negro woman named Ann, 28, for $1350.
27 Dec 1859   Jacob Shlenker
                               J. J. Loper
Witnesses: W. A. Glasson, H. Regenburg
Recorded 28 Dec 1859

Book J, P 74
Before me, William C. Smith, Parish Recorder, came John Odom, who declares that he has sold to Pinkney Odom a negro boy, Major, 17, for $1800.
1 Dec 1859   John Odom
                               Pinkney Odom
Witnesses: John King, Josephus McGough
Recorded 31 Dec 1859

Book J, P 82
Received of Royal K. Love payment for slaves as indicated. For Dinah, 60, $300. For Matilda, 26, $1200. For Corene, 10, $900.
21 May 1859   E. D. Galbraith
                               Royal K. Love
Witnesses: J. E. Milburn, Jared Robinson
Recorded 14 Jan 1860

Book J, P 102
Before me, William C. Smith, Parish Recorder, appeared R. K. Love, who states he has sold to Alexander Ambleton 4 negro slaves for the sum of $2250: Lotty and child; Catherine, and Luck, 30.
26 Jan 1860   R. K. Love

Alexander Ambleton
Witnesses: Jared Robinson, Daniel M. Payne
Recorded 26 Jan 1860

Book J, P 117
Know all men that I, Etheldred Sled, have sold to James M.
Underwood a slave boy named Nathan, 24, for $1500.
4 Jan 1860   E. D. Sled
                                        J. M. Underwood
Witnesses: H. Regenburg, E. Brunner
Recorded 6 Feb 1860

Book J, P 130
V. I. Bird appeared before me, Wm C. Smith, Parish Recorder, to
declare he has purchased from James M. Underwood, a negro slave,
named Nathan, 14, for $1700.
16 Jul 1860   James M. Underwood
                                       V. I. Bird
Witnesses: B. F. Dillard H. C. Glasson
Recorded 16 Jul 1860

Book J, P 150
Before me, William C. Smith, Parish Recorder, came Pricella Bledsoe,
who declares she has sold to E. D. Sled a slave woman named Mary,
35, for $900.
13 Feb 1860   Pricella Bledsoe
                                       E. D. Sled
Witnesses: J. G. Taylor, J. H. Cann
Recorded 13 Feb 1860

Book J, P 156
Pursuant to an order of the 12th Judicial Court, I, John T. Matthews,
have sold at public auction slaves of the estate of John Matthews,
deceased. To Sterling C. Lee for $1305, Burton, 47. To Daniel
Abbott, for $1230, Mason, 49. To James Matthews, Jarrett, 11, for
$850. To Joseph Telford for $1296.30, Eleck, 14. To Joseph Abbott,
for $2905, Polly, 38, and children, Mary Ann, 8, Caroline, 6, Joel, 4,
Robert, 2, and infant (not named). To John T. Matthews for $825,
Hannah, 16.

28 Nov 1859   John T. Matthews, administrator
Witnesses: John L. Barrett, H. M. Barrett
Recorded 23 Feb 1860

Book J, P 166
Received of Savory O. Larch the sum of $700 in payment for a slave
boy named Stephen, 8.
14 Feb 1860   Julia A. Arbothenot, wife
                                         of Henry D. Downs
                                         S. O. Larch
Witnesses: W. W. Guthrie, E. H. Ward
Recorded 28 Feb 1860

Book J, P 180
In consideration of the sum of $1220, I have sold to Franklin A.
Phelps a negro boy named Henry, 10.
8 Mar 1860   Martin Hendrick
                                         Franklin A. Phelps
Witnesses: James P. McGough, Malissa A. Hendrick
Recorded 8 Mar 1860

Book J, P 185
Be it remembered that by an order of the 12th Judicial Court, I, John
L. Barrett, administrator of the estate of John A. Bayless, have sold at
auction to highest bidders certain slaves. Sold to Nancy D. Bayless,
Sally, 8, $1165. To Martha P. Bayless, Moses, 15, for $1175.
14 Mar 1860   Nancy D. Bayless
Witnesses: H. M. Barrett
Recorded 14 Mar 1860

Book J, P 187
Be it remembered that in pursuance of an order of the 12th Judicial
Court, authorizing sale of property of Carson and Bayless, I, Nancy D.
Bayless, sold slaves of the estate as indicated. To Wm. Glasson,
Wallace, 33, for $1000. To James W. Underwood, John, 21, for
$1530. To J. R. Thompson, Washington, 28, for $1525. To John
West, Edmund, 32, for $1020. To Moses S. Carson, Rachel (no age
shown) for $925. To Cullen Edwards, for $531, Caroline, 38. To
David M. Jameson, Lewis, 30, for $1100.

14 Mar 1860   Nancy D. Bayless
Witnesses: H. M. Barrett, Thomas C. Lewis
Recorded 14 Mar 1860

Book J, P 194
Know all men that I have sold to Wesley W. Walker a slave girl named
Dicy, 12, for $1100.
31 Dec 1858   Solomon Feazel
                                     W. W. Walker
Witnesses: S. C. Lee, Britten Honeycutt
Recorded 31 Dec 1858

Book J, P 194
Received of F. L. Cook, the sum of $400 for a negro woman named
Polly, 40.
14 Feb 1860   G. W. Albritton
                                     F. L. Cook
Witnesses: J. R. Albritton (second name obscure)
Recorded 28 Mar 1860

Book J, P 227
Before me, William C. Smith, Parish Recorder, appeared Lucretia
Jones, who declares she has sold to V. I. Bird a negro slave named
Bob for $1400.
13 Apr 1860   Lucretia Jones (her mark: X)
                                     V. I. Bird
Witnesses: W. E. Jones, T. Holloway
Recorded 13 Apr 1860

Book J, P 233
Know ye all men that for the sum of $1400, I, J. J. Loper, have sold to
Brunner and Shlenker a negro slave named Ann. (No age shown.)
17 Apr 1860   J. J. Loper
Witnesses: Dan T. Head, R. Stanback
Recorded 17 Apr 1860

Book J, P 254
Pursuant to an order of the 12th Judicial Court, we, Delano L. Hicks
and Wm. B. McCormick, legal experts, have sold at auction to highest

bidders slaves of the estate of Thomas B. Graham, late of Alabama. Lot #1: Isaac, 50, to John A. Graham, for $1050. Lot #2: Gilly, 40, and infant child, Nelly, to Margaret J. Manning for $1500. Lot #3: Henry, 13, to Evander Graham, for $1350. Lot #4: Eliza, 11, and Laura, 5, to Isabella A. Mattox for $400. Lot #5: Randall, 7, to A. D. McDuffie for $800.

4 May 1860   Delano L. Hicks

Witnesses: W. C. Smith, David Calks (his mark: X)
Recorded 27 May 1860

Book J, P 268
Be it remembered that before me, William C. Smith, Parish Recorder, appeared Allen M. Callaway, who declares he has sold to Samuel W. Taylor, the following negro slaves: Merritt, a boy, 12, and Ennis, a boy, 10, for $2200.

24 May 1860   Allen M. Callaway
                            Saml W. Taylor

Witnesses: F. H. Carr, D. M. Wright
Recorded 24 May 1860

Book J, P 272
Know ye all men that in consideration of the sum of $2650, we, Carey and McMerty, have sold to Alex M. Taylor, 2 negro slaves, Kitty, 26, and James, 18.

28 Mar 1860   S. J. Carey
                            John McMerty
                            Alex M. Taylor

Witnesses: F. H. Carr, William Taylor
Recorded 28 May 1860

Book J, P 278
Before me, William C. Smith, Parish Recorder, appeared Lucretia Jones, who states she has given to her daughter, Ana A. Jones, a slave boy named Wesley, 14, valued at $1100.

13 Jun 1860   Lucretia Jones
                            (her mark: X), tutrix

Witnesses: R. W. Futch, A. M. Callaway
Recorded 13 Jun 1860

Book J, P 290
In consideration of the sum of $600, I, John Dean, of Hickory Grove, have sold to Franklin Armstrong a girl, Polly, 18, and a boy, Pharoah, 2.

24 Nov 1843   John Dean
                               Franklin Armstrong
Witness: George Robinson
Recorded 24 Nov 1843

Book J, P 305
In consideration of the love and affection I have for my children, I convey to them slave property bought of James B. Eckles in Union Parish, Louisiana. To my son, Thomas W. Anderson, negroes Stephen, Celia, Ben, and Lucy. To my daughter, Mary Alethea Boswell, negroes Jeff and his wife, Ann, and her 2 children, Sterling and Lipa. To my son, Frank James Anderson, negroes Washington, Moses and Mary. (No ages shown.)

2 Mar 1860   James Anderson
Witnesses: A. C. Gibson, Henry Moor (Deed was executed in Upson County, Georgia, recorded in Union Parish 20 Aug 1860).

Book J, P 326
Be it known to all men that I, Maria R. Dozier, in consideration of the sum of $600, have sold to Harriett R. Dozier a negro slave named John, 24.

1 Apr 1856   Maria R. Dozier
                               Harriett R. Dozier
Witness: William C. Dozier (Deed was executed in Washington County, Alabama, recorded in Union Parish 1 Apr 1856.

Book J, P 332
Know ye all men that we, John Williams and Rosetta Williams, in consideration of the sum of $1700, have sold to Rachel Acree a negro slave, Silas, 25.

19 Sep 1860   John Williams
                               Rosetta Williams
                               Rachel Acree
Witnesses: D. B. Acree, F. B. Williams
Recorded 19 Sep 1860

Book J, P 343
Know all men by these presents that we, Catherine Caver, spouse of the late Henry Caver, with Ann R. Caver, wife of Joseph Gates, Martha C. Caver, wife of Reuben Wall, Y. Columbus Caver, and J. L. B. Caver, all agree to dividing negro slaves, by drawing lots, value as shown. Ann R. Caver drew Lot #1 (Tenor, a man, $1100, Charles, $1100, and William, $800). Martha C. Caver drew Lot #2 (Kitty, $1000, Frank, $900, Wesley, $400, and Margret, $400). Mrs. Catherine Caver drew Lot #3 (Silvey, $1400, David, $700, Eliza, $400, George, $300, and Sara, $200). Y. Columbus Caver drew Lot #4 (Dianah, $700, John, $1000, Tom, $700, Ann, $350, Alfred, $350, and Allen, $200). J. L. B. Caver drew Lot #5 (Bob, $1500, Alson, $1000, and Mary, $800). (No ages shown.)

11 Jun 1860	Catherine Caver (her mark: X)
	Ann R. Gates
	Martha C. Caver
	J. L. B. Caver
	Yancy C. Caver

Witnesses: John L. Barrett, M. E. Daniel
Recorded 5 Oct 1860

Book J, P 348
Know ye all men that I, Wm. D. Cooper, have sold to E. O. G. Andrews, for the sum of $1400, Minerva, 10, and Manda, 6.

8 Oct 1860	Wm. D. Cooper
	E. O. G. Andrews

Witnesses: M. E. Daniel, J. A. Harrell
Recorded 8 Oct 1860

Book J, P 357
Know ye all men that I, J. B. Ivey, have sold to John G. Hollis, for total sum of $2000, Peggy, 40, and her children, Nice, 8, Herod, 6, Sallie, 4, Peggy, 2, and Abe, 1.

4 Feb 1860	J. B. Ivey
	J. G. Hollis

Witnesses: J. G. Sessions, John W. Scott
Recorded 10 Oct 1860

Book J, P 358
Know all men by these presents that I, Robert J. Willson, have sold to
J. J. Loper a negro man named Steven, 25, for $1750.
11 May 1860   Robert J. Willson
                                     J. J. Loper
Witnesses: D. Gresham, Charles Delery
Recorded 10 Oct 1860

Book J, P 400
In pursuant of an order by the 12th Judicial Court, I, Felix Hargis,
administrator of the estate of Gabriel N. Benson, deceased, have sold
to highest bidders slaves of the estate as indicated. To Gabriel R.
Plummer, Wiley and his wife, Mary, for $435, Bob, 61, for $336, and
Silas for $1690. To Wiley Cammock, Isom, a man, 30, for $1500,
Martha and her children (no ages shown) for $1500, and Elisha, 22,
for $1295. To William A. Glasson, Jesse, for $1450. To James Jeter,
Peter, 10, for $600. To Daniel Shaw, Cynthia, (no age shown) for
$1035. To Robert Tabor, Clarissa, for $800. To Elias George,
Reuben, 20, and Alick, 19, for $3150.
3 Dec 1860   F. G. Hargis, Adm
Witnesses: F. H. Carr, B. B. Thomas
Recorded 11 Dec 1860

Book J, P 418
Know all men by these presents that we, Robert Stewart, of Alabama,
and George D. Stewart, of Union Parish, Louisiana, agree to partition
of the estate of Elizabeth A. Plyant, deceased, wife of Henry Plyant.
Robert Stewart received slaves, Sarah, and children, Jinney, Winney,
Taylor, Gov, Judge, and West (no ages shown), value $5300. The
second heir, George D. Stewart, received same value in cash.
29 Dec 1860   Henry Plyant, adm
                                     Robert Stewart
                                     George D. Stewart
Witnesses: Elijah Tabor, A. W. Harris
Recorded 29 Dec 1860

Book J, P 431

Know ye all men that I, D. S. Easley, for the sum of $1800, have sold to Martha Temple, wife of William Temple, negro slaves, to wit, Winney, 28, and her child, Howard (no age shown), and Lewis, 10.

14 Dec 1859   D. S. Easely
                          Martha Temple
Witnesses: E. E. Poole, D. W. Easley
Recorded 14 Dec 1860

Book J, P 483
Pursuant to an order of the 12th Judicial Court, I, M. F. Simmons, administrator of the estate of Martha F. Davis, deceased, have sold negro slaves at public auction to highest bidders as shown. To William E. Davis, Mary, for $1400. To James H. Davis, a woman, Sarah, for $1300. To Thomas G. Davis, Jane and her children, Lucy, Noah, and infant (no name shown) for $1230. (No ages shown.)

11 Mar 1860   M. F. Simmons
Witnesses: H. Regenburg, W. A. Glasson
Recorded 12 Mar 1861

Book J, P 491
Before me, William C. Smith, Parish Recorder, appeared Allen M. Callaway, who declares he has sold to J. C. Manning the slave named Joe, for $1000. (No age shown.)

20 Mar 1861   Allen M. Callaway
                          J. C. Manning
Witnesses: M. Little, A. H. Granger
Recorded 20 Mar 1861

Book J, P 499
Be it remembered that we, Anderson Cabray and Elizabeth Cabray Reppond, have sold to Emanuel Gross and Brother, a negro woman named Judah, about 40 years old for the sum of $600.

20 Mar 1860   Anderson Cabray
                          Elizabeth Cabray Repond
                          Emanuel Gross and Brother
Witnesses: Henry Gross, Larkin Lewis
Recorded 25 Mar 1860

Book J, P 501

Before me, William C. Smith, Parish Recorder, came heirs of the estate of John F. Burford, deceased, who agreed to partition property, assisted by Legal Experts John and Alexander Taylor. Lot #1, slaves: John, for $1275, Louisa, for $1300, Vince, for $875, Amanda, for $650, and Leonard, for $530, sold to Elizabeth Baker, wife of W. S. McGough. Lot #2, Floid, for $1220, Hannah, for $1075, Henry, for $425, Sally, for $950, and George, for $775, sold to John T. Burford, minor, signed for by Jordan G. Taylor, tutor. Lot #3, London, for $1220, Cook, for $1100, Thomas, for $650, Mahala, for $950, and Winney, for $700, sold to Sally A. Smith, wife of William P. Smith. Lot #4, Bob, for $1200, Lubey and child, for $1250, Wilson, for $400, Charley, for $450, Peter, for $350, Will, for $600, and Rudy, for $300, to William M. Burford, minor, signed for by Joseph G. Baker, tutor. Lot #5, Ben, for $1250, Sophia, and child for $1325, Clarisy, for $300, Benny/Berry? for $500, Esther, for $1075, sold to Robert B. Burford, minor, signed for by William C. Hall, tutor. (No age shown.)

28 Mar 1861   John Taylor
                     Alexander Taylor

Witnesses: H. Regenburg, A. Thomas
Recorded 28 Mar 1861

Book J, P 515
Know ye all men that I, Martin Hendrick, have sold to Alex M. Taylor for $800, a slave boy named Joseph, 10.

7 Mar 1861   Martin Hendrick
                     Alex M. Taylor

Witnesses: H. Regenburg, E. B. Smith
Recorded 4 Apr 1861

Book J, P 517
Received of T. J. Jones the sum of $438 in payment for a negro girl, 3, named Sidney.

8 Apr 1861   John Nolen
                     T. J. Jones

Witnesses: Thomas Pilgreen, F. W. McClendon
Recorded 8 Apr 1861

Book J, P 518

Pursuant to an order of the 12th Judicial Court, I, Elizabeth Harvey, administrator of the estate of John Harvey, deceased, have sold at public auction to Campbell Lassiter a slave man named Jay, for the sum of $500.
8 Apr 1861   Elizabeth Harvey, admnx
Witnesses: John L. Barrett, W. A. Darby
Recorded 18 Apr 1861

Book J, P 567
Be it remembered that before me, by an order of the 12th Judicial Court, appeared Sidney H. Griffin, administrator of the estate of William T. Gilbert, deceased, who declares he has sold at auction slaves of the estate. Mary Ann and child, to E. D. Sled, for $1500. Jane and her 3 children, to Brunner and Shlenker, for $2400. (No ages shown).
11 Jul 1861   Sidney H. Griffin
Witness: Wm. C. Smith, Recorder
Recorded 11 Jul 1861

Book J, P 568
Know all men that I, Alexander M. Taylor, have sold to Jordan G. Taylor slaves, viz, John Talbot, 18, for $1200, and Sarah, 21, for $1200.
29 Jun 1861   Alex M. Taylor
                                   J. G. Taylor Jr
Witnesses: Josephus McGough, L. Cooper
Recorded 12 Jul 1861

Book J, P 571
Know ye all men that I, William Jones, for the sum of $1182, have sold to Wright Sherrard, Jr a negro slave named Mary, 17, and her child (name and age not shown).
15 Jul 1861   William O. Jones
                                   Wright Sherrard Jr
Witnesses: Walter D. Mitchell, O. B. Sholars
Recorded 15 Jul 1861

Book J, P 579

Know ye all men that I, Thomas M. Smith, have sold to Nelia Vines certain slaves, to wit, Edie, 18 and her children, Francis, 4, and Frederick, 18 months, for the sum of $1500.

9 Jan 1856   T. M. Smith
                                        Nelia Vines
Witnesses: O. B. Hill, D. M. Jameson
Recorded 25 Jul 1861

Book J, P 580
Be it remembered that I, Elizabeth Reppond, have given to heirs of Sarah Cabray estate, slaves as follows: to Anderson W. Cabray, Ann, 11. To Elizabeth F. Cabray, a girl, Sine, 16. By order of the 12th Judicial Court.

17 Aug 1861   Elizabeth Reppond
Witnesses: E. A. Reppond, Saml Smith
Recorded 19 Aug 1861

Book J, P 590
By order of the 12th Judicial Court, I, Wesley W. Guthrie, acting Deputy Sheriff, have transferred to W. C. Carr the following negro slaves (no value shown): Nelson, 55, Charlott, 42, Mary, 40 and her son, Jonathan, 3, Joe, 16, George, 14, Fanny, 40, Angeline, 8, Steve, 4, and Andy, 18.

9 Sep 1861   Wesley W. Guthrie
                               W. C. Carr
Witnesses: B. F. Dillard, M. S. Carson
Recorded 19 Sep 1861

Book J, P 596
In consideration of the sum of $1450, I, John G. Stocks, have sold to Edmund O. G. Andrews, a negro man named Amos, 25.

14 Jul 1859   John G. Stocks
                               E. O. G. Andrews
Witnesses: John B. Eckles, John D. Buckley
Recorded 28 Sep 1860

Book J, P 599

By order of the 12th Judicial Court, I, William C. Carr, administrator of the estate of Sylvanus Shepherd, deceased, sold to A. W. McCormick the slave boy, Granderson, 12, for the sum of $1200.

5 Feb 1859	Wm. C. Carr
	A. W. McCormick

Witnesses: Benjamin C. Harrison, James H. McBroom
Recorded 1 Oct 1861

Book J, P 608
Be it remembered by order of the 12th Judicial Court I, Berry Fuller, Sheriff, have sold to William A. Glasson, a slave named Moses (or Mose) for $466. (No age shown.)

9 Oct 1861	Berry Fuller
	W. A. Glasson

Witnesses: M. S. Carson, D. Arent
Recorded 17 Oct 1861

Book K, P 16
Know ye all men that in consideration of the sum of $1200, I have sold to W. W. Bennett the slave, Rufus. (Age not shown.)

30 Dec 1861	Margaret Bennett
	W. W. Bennett

Witnesses: A. J. Bennett, Y. O. S. Webster
Recorded 30 Dec 1861

Book K, P 24
Before me, William C. Smith, Parish Recorder, appeared Margaret Bennett, whose name before marriage was Margaret Winn, who states she has given to Alexander Bennett, a minor son of William W. Bennett, which Alexander Bennett is her grandchild, a slave, Hardy, passing by the nickname of Sam, 15, which boy she appraises at $300.

3 Jan 1962	Margaret Bennett
	W. W. Bennett, natural tutor

Witnesses: R. G. Pleasant, J. J. Hammons
Recorded 4 Jan 1862

Book K, P 30

Received of G. W. Stripling the sum of $650 in payment for a female slave girl named Sinday, 17.

20 Jan 1855   Arthur Stripling

                                             G. W. Stripling

Witnesses: A. Merrell, J. H. Hooker

Recorded 29 Jan 1862

Book K, P 39

Before me, Wm C. Smith, Parish Recorder, came Absolom Wade, who declares he has sold to James L. Wade a slave woman named Candis for the sum of $1100 (No age shown.)

24 Feb 1862   Absolom Wade

                                             James L. Wade

Witnesses: Elisha P. Bolton, William Hopkins

Recorded 24 Feb 1862

Book K, P 75

Received of Joseph G. King the sum of $3500, payment for negro slaves, to wit, Charity, 24 and children, Henry, 9, Frances, 6, and Elick, 2.

28 Feb 1862   John R. Auld

                                             Joseph G. King

Witnesses: William R. Albritton, James W. Auld

Recorded 10 Mar 1862

Book K, P 146

Know ye all men that I have sold to Sarah Thompkins a slave girl named Clarrissa, 20, and her child, James, for $1200.

11 Dec 1862   Elias George Sr

                                             Sarah Thompkins

Witnesses: John L. Barrett, John Hendish

Recorded 11 Dec 1862

Book K, P 201

Know ye all men by these presents that I, H. P. Anderson, have sold to D. Arent, a negro slave named Joe, 21, for the sum of $2100.

5 Jun 1863   H. P. Anderson

                                             D. Arent

Witnesses: W. S. McGough, Asa Thomas

Recorded 5 Jun 1863

Book K, P 208
Before me, Wm C. Smith, Parish Recorder, appeared Frances L. Brown, who states she has sold to John Eubanks a slave named Jude, 22, and her children, Easter, 3, and Mack, 2, for $2600.
13 Jul 1863   Frances L. Brown
                                        Jno B. Eubanks
Witnesses: W. S. McGough, Rueben J. Ham
Recorded 13 Jul 1863

Book K, P 210
Before me, Wm C. Smith, Notary Public, appeared John B. Eubanks, who states he has sold to George A. J. Brown, a negro man named Sam, 35, for $2000.
13 Jul 1863   John B. Eubanks
                                        G. A. J. Brown
Witnesses: R. J. Ham, W. S. McGough
Recorded 13 Jul 1863

Book K, P 220
We, Frederick H. Carr and John M. Gulley, Legal Experts, have made a partition of slaves of the estate of Eliza A. Rossiter, deceased, by order of the 12th Judicial Court. George M. M. Rossiter, surviving husband of Elizabeth Ann Rossiter, drew Lot #1, as owner of slaves, to wit, Green, a man, 37, value $1200, Jim, a boy, 8, value $500, and Jane, 8, value $350. George Rossiter drew Lot #2, for Revs, a man, 26, value $1500, and Em, a girl, 14, value $700. Armand D. Watters drew Lot #3, for Bette, 30, and her children, Lucy, 3, Ann, 5, and Charles, 8, total value $2100. Jefferson B. Rossiter drew Lot #4 for Mariah, 24, and her child, Mary, 6 months, value $1200, and Wiley, 12, value $800. Harriett D. Webb drew Lot #5 for Violet, 19, value $1000, Wiley, 10, value $550, and Jerry, 11, value $600. William W. Aulds drew Lot #6 for Rose, 13, value $800, Ellen, 12, value $650, and Burrel, a boy, 15, value $800.
14 Aug 1863   F. H. Carr
                                        J. M. Gulley
Witnesses: B. F. Smith, P. H. McVicker
Recorded 18 Aug 1863

Book K, P 228
Be it known that I, Pereby Barnett, have sold to John W. Duty, 2 slaves, Willis, 47, and Olly, a woman, 47, for the sum of $3000.
10 Jul 1863   Pereby Barnett
                            John W. Duty
Witnesses: R. G. Pleasants, W. J. Oliver
Recorded 20 Aug 1863

Book L, P 33
In consideration of the sum of $3250, lawful money of the Confederate States, we, John A. Leache and Sarah Leache, have sold to John N. Duty a negro slave named Albert, 40.
4 Feb 1864   J. A. Leache
                         John N. Duty
Witnesses: A. W. Harris, R. L. Jones
Recorded 4 Feb 1864

Book L, P 42
By order of the 12th Judicial Court, I, John Phelps, administrator of the estate of David Rabun, deceased, have sold to James Gibson, a negro woman, named Sylla, 41, for the sum of $700.
19 Feb 1864   John Phelps (his mark: X)
                        James Gibson (his mark: X)
Witnesses: R. M. Futch, W. C. Lee
Recorded 19 Feb 1864

Book L, P 69
In consideration of the sum of $500 I, George W. Dutton, have sold to Washington S. Davis a negro boy called Peter, 4.
4 Apr 1864   George W. Dutton
                        Washington S. Davis
Witnesses: Levi Dearman, Arthur Bearden (his mark: X)
Recorded 21 May 1864

Book L, P 76
Know ye all men that I, John A. Ross, in consideration of the sum of $2500, have sold to Elias George a negro slave named Peter. (No age shown.)

30 May 1864   John A. Ross
                                     Elias George
Witnesses: J. J. Loper, Lou Roper
Recorded 31 May 1864

Book L, P 94
Received of Amanda Norris the sum of $800 in payment for a slave
girl named Martha, 10.
7 Sep 1864   D. M. Wright
                                    Amanda Norris
Witnesses: J. G. Wright, William C. Smith
Recorded 7 Sep 1864

Book L, P 109
Before me, William C. Smith, Notary Public, appeared Isaac Cole,
who declares that he has this day granted and conveyed to the State of
Louisiana, a certain negro man, Edmund, 22, to have and to hold unto
the said State of Louisiana forever. This sale is made in consideration
of the sum of $1600.
14 Apr 1865   Isaac Cole
                                    Wm. C. Smith
Witnesses: William H. Toler, Oliver P. Smith
Recorded 14 Apr 1865

Book L, P 291
Pursuant to order by the 12th Judicial Court, I, John Taylor, executor
of the estate of James Taylor, deceased, have sold to highest bidders
negro slaves of the estate. To William Pearson, Ellick, for $1525 and
Jack, for $1500. To David Nolan, Jerry, for $300. To James C.
Reynolds, Edmund, Jane and child, Gilly and child for $4920. To J. M.
Callaway, the woman, Spincer for $1850. To Wesley J. Baker,
Charley, for $2000. To John E. Green, David, for $1900. To H. C.
Glasson, the boy Bird, for $1050. To James Simmons, Martin, $3095.
(No ages shown.)
1 Dec 1860   John Taylor, Executor
Witnesses: N. Honeycutt, M. L. Barrett
Recorded 2 Dec 1860

Index
Slaveholders and Others

ABBOTT, Daniel 149 Daniel J 17
  Daniel Joseph 18 Joseph 149
  Sarah Ann 83
ABSENT, Charles 96 Charles M
  22
ACREE, D B 153 Daniel B 35
  Rachel 153
ADAMS, W W 56
AGERTON, Riley 132
ALBRITTON, G W 151 George
  W 19 J R 151 William 11
  William R 19 161
ALFORD, Green B 22
ALLEN, David E 54 Nancy 54 57
  Samuel 52
AMBLETON, Alexander 144
  148 149
ANDERSON, Eliza Allice 43
  Frank James 153 George 30
  H P 47 50 62 86 161 Henry
  P 12 43 47 50 James 153
  Sarah 43 Thomas W 24 153
  William 20 William Henry 43
ANDREWS, E O G 17 154 159
  Edmund O G 159 J T B 16
  130 146 John R 70 Martha
  M 70 84 R H 84 113 128
  Robert H 71 113 W A 116
ANNISETT, Andrew 31
  Charlotte 31 Elijah 31 Eliza
  D 31 Jesse 31 Martha 31
  Virginia 31
ARBOTHENOT, Julia A 150
ARCHER, John 12 38

ARENT, D 160 161 Dave 147
  David 127 131 134
ARMSTRONG, A 71 85
  Archibald 85 91 93 F M 101
  Franklin 153 M 67
ARRINGTON, John V 123
ATKINSON, William 61
ATWELL, John 74
AULD, James W 161 John R 161
  S A 107
AULDS, Adaline (Rossiter) 40 E
  M 57 80 130 Elijah M 101
  Elijah Michael 130 George
  W 40 James A 129 146 John
  19 John J 40 John R 129
  William A 40 William W 40
  162
AUSTON, John 47
AUTREY, Lewis 77
AUTRY, Absalom 7 W 145 W N
  6
AZWELL, Hiram 51
BAILEY, H 88 Hamilton 59
  Sarah 123
BAKER, Bright 9 Elizabeth 157
  Jack 9 John 38 John E 13 38
  John W 38 Joseph 85 89 100
  132 133 142 Joseph G 157
  Mary 9 Rebecca 86 Robert T
  J 92 W I Q 30 92 Wesley J
  164
BALEY, Charles H 47
BALL, W J 88

165

BARHAM, John A 5 40 John F
40 Martha 40 William F 40
BARKER, H J 48
BARMOORE, H 8
BARNETT, F 5 Pereby 163
BARR, Harriet 58 S M 58
BARRETT, H M 139 142 150
151 J S 122 John L 12 95
119 122 132 139 142 150
154 158 161 John S 117 M L
164
BARRON, H C 18 20 James 20
BARRY, Charles 91
BARTLET, H C 78
BARTON, C T 52 82 84 87 102
108 112 E J 97 Eliza 52 97
BASS, Richard 101 Uriah 14 100
121
BATES, William 47 A 14
BAYLESS, A T 12 J A 125 Jno
A 86 117 John A 35 50 86
99 105 109 117 125 126 150
Martha 35 Martha P 150
Nancy D 35 150
BEAIRD, John W 59 Zelphia 59
BEARD, William M 14
BEARDEN, A 134 Arthur 134
163 G W 87
BECK, A 8 Charles 127
BENNET, John 114
BENNETT, A J 160 Alexander
160 Harriett B 138 J M 3
John 138 John J 116
Margaret 138 160 Nancy 123
Nancy C 114 116 138 W W
160 William 3 William W
123 138 160
BENSON, G N 135 Gabriel N 23
42 155

BETTERTON, N 87
BEVIL, Adline 3
BILBERRY, E B 24 E G 142 J G
16 99 McDual 33 McDuel 99
BIRD, Ezra 30 Nancy Courtney
30 V I 56 59 65 71 93 102
104 109 111 114 117 122
124 128 131 133 136 138
142 145 149 151 Valin I 96
104 115 William 24 30
BLACK, James H 45 Reuben D
130
BLEDSOE, Moses W 56 Pricella
149
BOATRIGHT, John 45 101
Powhatten 65
BOATWRIGHT, John 125
BOLTON, E P 4 Elisha P 161
BOND, William F 55 56 William
F 73 Wm F 73
BOSWELL, Mary Alethea 153
BRADFORD, Thomas 79
BRADY, George W 53
BRANTLEY, Elizabeth 14 31 94
121 Jesse 31 59 Thomas 31
94 123 Thos 94
BRAZEL, R 18
BRAZZEL, F 106 109
BREED, Avery 53 58 61
BREWSTER, Elizabeth 44 Hiram
8 43 James M 44 William 9
43 44
BRIGGS, David B 64 96
BROOKS, S M 18
BROTHERS, A M 8
BROWN, B W 95 96 113 Elijah
W 54 F L 132 Frances L 162
G A J 162 George A J 162
Lewis 126 W H 131 W W 3

BRUNNER, E 149 Emanuel 124
G 128 L 104 116 126 127
131 Lazarus 12 104 124
BRUTON, N D M 93 Nancy 128
Reddick P 12 W D M 24 33
118 128
BRYAN, A R 75 D A 105
Florida C 66 H B 59 H R 66
68 75 77 80 89 90 113 Henry
R 66 77 90 111 Lucien 66 N
M 66 68 69 70 71 77 78 80
83 88 90 98 N R 59
Needham M 59 68 80 90 W
R 70 68 83
BRYANT, H R 58 James R 133
John H 46 Mary A 133 Mary
E 34 Sarah H 34
BUCHANAN, C 11
BUCKLEY, H L 16 John D 159
BURFORD, John F 16 37 157R,
John F 37 John T 157 Robert
37 Robert B 157 Sarah A 37
William 37 William M 157
BURKE, Gideon H 96
BUSH, W C 9 J V 65
BUTLER, John J 53
CABRAY, Anderson 156
Anderson W 159 Elizabeth F
159 Sarah 159
CABREARD, Sarah Grammont
77
CABRIL, G 22
CALDERWOOD, John 137
CALDWELL, Robert J 95 132
CALK, E G 120
CALKS, David 152
CALLAHAN, John B 137
CALLAWAY, A M 121 122 129
136 142 145 152 Allan M 12

136 152 156 Emily A 99
Emily Ann 99 Frances 99 J
M 164 John C 10 L C 10 91
92 103 136 Larkin C 91 92
W S 146 Wm G 99
CALVERT, Mary Jane 125
CAMMOCK, Wiley 155
CAMPBELL, John M 58
CANN, Harriett C 63 J H 149
CAPP, William J 109
CAREY, S J 152
CARGEL, James 19
CARR, A A 121 Allen 28 94 96
105 107 118 126 131 139
Allen C 28 F H 13 118
132-134 152 155 162
Frederick H 162 Sarah 57
Susan 28 W C 33 46 57 80
159 W H 96 William C 28 34
160 William Cleaton 13 Wm
C 160
CARROLL, F M 17 G R 84
CARSON, Elizabeth 35 H M 12
James H 35 72 105 James S
99 L H 110 M S M S 99 117
133 159 160 M Steel 118
Moses 109 Moses S 36 105
150 W H 12 35 100 102 133
146 William H 129 Wm H
123
CARTER, John 9
CASKEY, J W 17
CAVER, Ann R 154 Catherine
154 Henry 154 J L B 154
Martha C 154 Y Columbus
154 Yancy C 154
CENAS, H B 91
CHANDLER, Lewis 47
CHAPLIAN, Chichester 49

CHAPMAN, S 23 W 87 William 87
CHRISTIAN, J D 77 Joseph D 77
CLARK, C C 17 Charles 124 J R 5 Mary C 40 Susan 124 William A 123
CLARKE, Charles N V 145
CLAYTON, G W 20 38
COKER, Asa 5
COKER, W H 128
COLE , Mary 110 Isaac 164 Matilda 33 Reuben 123
COLESON, James A 101 James W 108 Prudentia 101
COLLINS, Eli 87 Eli L 66 90 William A 143
COLSTON, James 19
COLVIN, C H 71 Daniel 53 Daniel Jr 27 Daniel Sr 27 Jeptha 27 John C 7 Mary J 71
COMMANDER, A 91
COOK, Benjamin P 32 D P A 50 52 108 Don P A 74 Don Pedro Acquilla 24 50 52 Elizabeth Jane 138 F L 12 110 151 Robert 46 48 Wiley 7 138
COOPER, A B 49 A J 49 Anna 27 C M 24 Elvina 49 Hiram 54 119 142 Hynson 125 J D 49 Jesse 27 L 24 158 Lexington 27 M B 85 Marshal Colombus 27 Martha Jane 27 125 Mary Jane 125 T L 147 T S 24 Thomas F 27 W D 147

William 145 William D 98 William O 27 Wm D 154
COURTNEY, A H 80
COX, G W 5 Thomas 11
CRANE, Edward 29 Timothy 29 88
CRANFORD, John M 92
CRAWFORD, A F 143 James M 4 30 Jemima 87 Jemima Harrison 30 John M 92 110 N S 11 W F 108 W H 11 Wm H 72
CREATH, J A 119 James A 16 39 93 94 Nancy J 39
CROW, John 22 39 Lucinda 39 Stephen R 39
CULBERTSON, John 11 95 103 L T 11 William H 11 103 Wm H 103
CULP, J G 10
CULVERHOUSE, Mary 137 William 88 97
CURTIS, John D 110
DACUS, C H 103
DANIEL, J J 60 85 M E 16 154
DARBY, A.C 38 D A 106 W A 61 63 64 67 72 80 84 107 122 131 139 141 142 158 William 38 William A 14 38 40 Wm 122 Wm A 122
DARDEN, Uriah M 74
DAVIS, B E 50 55 73 74 79 Benjamin E 31 53 56 73 Benjamin F 31 Columbus C 31 David E 59 George 73 J A G 78 J B 45 James H 156 John 45 John A G 45 78 John K 31 M 79 Malinda 56 67 Malinda D 73 Mark 78 79

Martha F 35 156 Mary
Frances 31 Nancy 8 O G 87
Susan 133 T L 24 Thomas G
156 Thomas I 31 W E 24 W
T 116 Walter A 31
Washington S 163 William E
35 156 William R 133
DAWKINS, Duncan D 16
DAWSON, D D 22 H B 69
DAY, John 84 Marshall 98
DEAN, E M 141 Hansford 117
Jesse 40 John 40 153 Richard
67 Sarah 15 142 William A
13 40
DEARING, Mary T 109 W L 17
William 130
DEARMAN, Levi 163
DEES, Elizabeth 67 J B 57 67
DEGRAFFENRIED, William 51
Wm 51
DELERY, Charles 155
DELK, D R 66 97 105 R 72
DELONEY, Manimus 51
DENNIS, Charles R 103 John
130
DENSON, Isaac 84 Lemuel 84
DICK, Mary 70
DICKENSON, G T 134
DICKERSON, Jackson 11
DILDY, Charles C 17
DILLARD, B F 70 73 75 81 85
149 159 B G 70 Benjamin F
13 145 Ellen 123 Jake 74 75
DIXON, John A 132 Mixon D 95
132 William H 95
DOATY, L A 19
DOBEY, H K 84
DONAGHAY, C 42
DONNELLY, John 45 46 49

DOTY, S A 142 William A 33
DOUGLASS, James A 131
DOUMAS, Jeremiah S 16
DOWNS, Henry D 150
DOZIER, Harriett C 63 Harriett
R 63 153 James A 63 90 91
Maria R 153 William C 153
DRAKE, Hervey 143 Reubin 56
DRIVER, Benjamin J 99
DUBOSE, Jeremiah 110 Wade H
110
DUNKIN, Foster H 55
DUNN, Stephen 59
DUTTON, George W 163
DUTY, John N 163 John W 163
EASELY, D S 156
EASLEY, D W 156
EASTERLING, Shadrack 48
Spencer H 48 William B 48
ECKLES, J B 16 James B 153
John B 159
EDMOND, William 118 Martha
A 42 Mary Jane 42 Nancy 34
Rosco 34 William J 34
EDMUNDS, Nancy 5
EDWARDS, C 14 Cullen 95 118
119 150 Cullen H 13 36 42
James 5 117 John 78 108 116
117 Miller 54 Nancy 140 R
14 Reuben 141
ELKINS, H K 17
ELLIS, B E 79 89 Benjamin C 10
Reuben 80 96 97 102 M T
97 Mary C 11 128 133
Reuben 63 64 80-83 84
86-91 128
ESSICK, H B 69 91 92 99 100
102 104 107 109 116 119
121 124 126 136

EUBANKS, Jno B 162 John 162
John B 162 W W C 62
EVANS, Nancy Marion 30 Wm
49
EVELL, William 78
EVERETT, G W 96 George 95
118 George W 33 J P 96
John P 21 95 96 128 130
Thomas M 21
FARMER, Permelia A 48
Benjamin F 10 28 35 41 121
125 John 28 John N 28 51 53
72 John W 53 Leah 28 Mary
41 Permelia Ann 48 Rachel
28 Rachel Acree 35 S M 81
Shepard 82 Susannah 28 W
W 28 45 48 49 102 104
William W 46
FARRAR, Samuel B 54
FARRIS, Elias 16
FARROW, J H 17 R F 21
William 18
FAUGHT, John 47 Susan 47
FEAZEL, George 129 Isiah S 39
J O 11 John 39 77 P 11
Philip 39 45 46 48 49 67 S
130 Sarah E 28 Solomon 4
28 39 46 49 85 88 117 121
122 125 151
FENNER, Sherrard McCall 50
FERGUSON, D G 137 E H 137
Samuel G 134
FERRELL, Thomas F 59
FINDLEY, Leroy 4 50 58 Leroy
H 74 T W 129 Wm C H 58
FLEMING, Anderson 107 Jane L
108 Neely 52
FLOURNOY, A F 141 J H 141

FORD, Alfred 84 B F 82
Benjamin 22 John M 8 41
John W 109 Nancy 18 S P 20
FOSTER, James M 135 Mary 68
T M 135
FOWLER, Richard 111
FOX, Wm 146
FOY, Eliza 70 71
FRANKLIN, Ethelbert S 51
FRILLSON, Henry 75 79
FULLER, A J 6 B 76 Berry 76
143 160 C Marion 6 Cynthia
6 D W 123 J G 107 Jeff 40
Jesse 28 107 Jesse G 5 Mary
28 Nancy 111 William E 28
FUNDERBURK, Deborah A 36
H 78 Henry 19 36
FUTCH, Allen 15 B W 144
David 146 R M 163 R W
152 Robert W 41
GALBRAITH, E D 148
GALBREATH, John 20
GASKILL, A D 3 Evans 3 Louisa
A 105
GASKINS, John 33
GATES, Ann R 154 Joseph 154
GATHRIGHT, James G 118
GEORGE, A B 78 Benjamin F 23
35 42 Elias 42 86 115 122
135 155 163 164 Elias Sr
161 Eliza 35 Martha Ann 23
35 W L 115 Washington E
35 Washington L 35
GERSEN, Henry 74 76
GIBSON, A C 153 B 56 Jacob 66
James 163
GILBERT, Charles S 38 Charles
H 14 James R 14 38 40 M A
19 Mary Ann 34 R M 38 40

Sidney H 34 T J 20 140
Thomas 14 Thomas F 38
William T 34 158
GILL, Mary J 103 W M 7
GILLCOATE, Azaniah 124
GLASS, Jesse W 98 Joel 98
GLASSON, F B 15 H C 78 95 99
102 116 119 122 149 164
Harriett 88 Harriett A 88
Hugh C 99 James B 81 W A
97 98 100 125 126 128 144
148 156 160 W C 89 William
A 88 92 155 160 William G
73 William H 13 35 William
L 42 Wm 150 Wm A 133
GLAZE, Jesse 124
GODLEY, Columbus 37
Elizabeth 37 James B 37
John M 21 37 Martha A 37
Mary A 37
GOLDSBY, M W 39 Miles W 21
122 Peter R 108
GOLSBY, P R 112 Peter R 112
GOODGER, D M 4 Martha 4
GOODWIN, George W 95 James
E 5 James M 38 Martha A 38
GOYNE, Davis 19 H Davis 119
Hiram D 84 100 J R 18 W J
18 134 Wm J 100
GRAHAM, E M 120 Evander
152 Evander M 36 George R
36 John A 36 152 Margaret J
36 Thomas B 36 152
Thomas E 36
GRANGER, A H 125 133 156
GRAVES, Lewis 83 Prudence 33
GRAY, John 15 17 Thomas 3
GRAYSON, A K 125

GREEN, Abner 98 Callaway 6 D
W 7 Elizabeth Ann 80 96
115 J E 108 J H 108 John 7
John B Jr 7 John E 24 112
130 134 164 John Ernal 130
Mary 76 77
GRESHAM, D 155 James 99
Louisa 33
GREY, John 132 Sarah 132
GRIFFIN, Ada 41 C H 12
Catherine E 41 Ellen 41
George W 29 James D 114
John William 27 John H 50
76 Julia Ann Temperence 27
Lorenzo A 27 Louisa S 29
Mariah 27 Martha Ann 76
Mary Ann 29 S H 20 Sidney
H 29 41 158 Thomas J 17 47
William Lorenzo Addison 27
GRISHAM, Dudley 115
GROOM, Elijah 59
GROSS, Emanuel 156 Henry 156
GUICE, James R 61 Joel 52 John
H 46
GULLEY, J H 18 J M 162 John
M 162 William L Sr 19
GUNTER, N W 141
GUTHRIE, W W 136 146 150
Wesley W 159
HAGEN, Hugh 64
HAILE, F 95 111 118 Fergurson
89 95 102 104 119
HALL, Anny 27 James 27 28
John 27 28 W C 18 William
C 27 28 157 Wm B 64
HAM, H H 145 Hillary H 110
Hillary Hub 19 R J 19 162
Rueben J 162 William 19 32
52 100

HAMILTON, Henry W 4
HAMMOCK, G A 99 John A 3
119 John S 6 Wiley J 42
HAMMOND, G A 69 86 George
A 70 73
HAMMONS, J J 160
HAND, Charles C 102 T M 102
112 Thomas M 95 99 102
111 118 137
HARGIS, Elizabeth A 40 Ella 40
F G 137 144 155 Felix 155
Felix G 23 40 Felix G Jr 40
HARPER, Henry W 129
HARRELL, Benjamin L 109 J A
154 J P 17
HARRIS, A W 3 155 163 D M
61 62 David M 47 Susan 121
HARRISON, Benjamin 30
Benjamin C 160 Jemima Ann
Ratliffe 30 Sarah 30 William
Allen 30
HART, James 94 147
HARVEY, Elizabeth 36 158 John
14 36 158
HAYES, A T 18 Jeremiah 127 S
T 120
HAYS, James 9 Jeremiah 20
HAYWOOD, George 67 George
W 68
HEAD, Dan T 151
HEARD, Emily Smith Traylor 29
George Felix 29 Joseph M 34
39 Mary 4 34 39 S S 6 S L
39 T M 71 Thomas Smith 27
29 William C 5
HEATH, Robert J 40
HENDERSON, I T 64 J T 80 J Y
98 John W 138 S T 80
William 114

HENDISH, John 161
HENDLEY, Cyrus B 54 Nancy
54
HENDRICK, David 30 32 45 52
54 55 79 David Jr 32
Elizabeth 75 James Martin 5
John 111 John W 63 66 71
77 111 M 16 Malissa A 150
Maria Louisa 47 Martin 67
71 100 150 157 Phoebc 32
111 Sarah A 77 Sara E 63
HENDRIX, Elizabeth 72 Hiram
72
HENRY, C J 6 Charles 42 James
27 James II 27 John F 27
Mary 42 Mary Alexander 27
Susan 27
HESTER, Randolph 64 Elizabeth
64 Elizabeth Y 92 J T 10
John 10 John J 8 John W 120
Randolph 64 S T 10
HICKS, D C 145 D L 104 Delano
L 151 152 Heremiah G 148
HILL, John 50 57 58 60 75 78 79
John G 64 Josiah 101 O B 20
123 124 130 142 159 Oliver
B 106 Oliver Bryan 103
HINDES, A D 53 M A 53 M L
53 Mitty Ellin 53
HINES, Felix 124 John H 98
Rhoda 98 Rhody H 98
HINTON, Thomas 82
HOBBS, Henry 77
HOBDAY, Benjamin J 8 Eliza 8
Jeanette 8
HODGE, C W 10
HOLADAY, Matilda 31
HOLLIDAY, John 144

HOLLIS, H G 140 J G 22 89 90
129 154 John 108 John G
154 T J 142
HOLLOWAY, George 30 James
L 30 Jane 30 John 16 T 151
William L 30
HOLT, Josiah 81
HONEYCUTT, Albert 72 Alfred
112 Austin 9 34 Britten 21
129 142 151 Eliza 34 George
W 67 89 Jesse 34 John 56
Mary 24 N 164 Susan Ann
Mixon 34
HOOKER, J H 161
HOPKINS, Ephriam 67 William 4
161
HOUGH, Wade H 45
HOWE, James W 137
HUEY, James 3d 48 John 47
HUFFMAN, Russell 7
HUGHS, Jeptha 60
HUNT, A J 127
HUTCHINSON, Abram 137
IKARD, M 91
IVEY, Hugh 105 J B 22 129 140
141 154 Nancy 33 Thomas
33 120 Thomas D 121 141
JAMESON, D M 140 159 David
M 20 36 129 150
JARMAN, E M 92 John D 78
Mary 69 Matilda 78
JEFFRIES, B R 63
JEMISON, Humphrey 51
JESSUP, George 14
JETER, James 22 42 155
JOHNSON, A M 118 A P 135 A
W 33 Elizabeth 27 J M 143
James D 94 James H 5 Job
27 M 63 96 Nicholas 94

Shadrick 130 Sherman 78
Theopholus 147 William R
122 123
JONES, Aaron M 94 Amy Ann
43 Ana A 152 Ann M 102 B
H 59 Berwell 70 Berwell H
57 65 Brice 70 Burrell H 31
C B 92 100 Delaware 33
Delaware S 43 E 16 J 100
107 J E 62 84 100 126 132
James 13 100 107 James E
52 54 55 66 77 84 88 90 107
121 125 126 131 Louisa 65
70 Lucretia 151 152 R L 163
Ralph 63 100 Richard 65 70
T J 157 Thomas D 68 W E
151 W O 68 69 83 90 93 106
107 113 William 158 William
O 8 33 43 68 69 72 89 93
100 107 158
KEENER, Stacy 10
KELLEY, Ann 119 Joel 55 56 73
John 119 John G 96 W G 64
William J 55
KELLY, J C 89 Joel P 36 John C
93 Malinda 31 Samuel S 58
Thomas B 110
KENNEDY, Permelia 27
KIDD, Albert A 72 J A 131 John
W 105 N A 72 114 Webb 72
114 Webb Jr 72
KILGORE, George A 13 Jane L
107 Julia A 107 Thomas 17
KILLAM, Camilla Lianda 31
Eliza Foy 31 James 31 James
Warren 31
KILLGORE, George 95 George
A 139

KING, Charles P 11 41 Henry 41
James 11 83 90 91 John 148
Joseph G 15 41 161 Mary 41
William 41
KITCHENS, Ansel 14
KNOX, George H 75
KOLB, James G 76 77 124 148 L
T 76
LAMBRIGHT, George 68 88
LANCER, Lewis 74
LANIER, Lewis 55
LANKFORD, Peter 136
LAPSTER, Charles 86
LARCH, L 77 Lucian 77 S O 119
122 128 133 150 Savory O
150
LARCHE, S O 95 117 121 127
130 Savory O 137 139
LARKEN, S J 58 Samuel J 58
LARKIN, J R 115 S J 91 S L 110
Samuel J 21 115 55 82 91 W
J 95
LASSITER, Campbell 65 66 69
158 H B 68 Henry 68 90
Henry B 66 59 97
LAWRENCE, Charles R 7
Charles W 146 W M 66 84
137 William M 7 51 74 76
Wm M 88
LEACH, John A 4
LEACHE, J A 163 John A 163
Sarah 163
LEE, A 21 Anderson 130 E 15 J
M 18 James E 54 66 John M
142 M B 128 M D 18
Richard 47 S C 13 139 142
151 Sterling C 149 W C 163
LEGGIN, James G 7 Louis 7
LEVI, M 135 Max 137

LEVISON, Abraham 80
LEWIS, John 54 Larkin 156
Nancy 12 Thomas C 117 151
LIGHT, Y K 17
LINDSAY, M W 109 Matthew
W 109 Whitfield 70
LITTLE, Catharine 147 George
15 139 147 M 19 156
LOCHE, Louisa C 147
LOCKHART, A H 87
LOCKWOOD, G W 4 Wesley W
16
LOPER, J J 115 122 135 147 148
151 155 164 John J 135 L P
23 Louisa 135
LOVE, Emilette 144 Emilette
Ambleton 144 James K 81
Mileet 79 R K 144 148 Royal
K 144 148 64 79 93 R R 113
LOVELADY, J S 6
LOW, B F 19
LOWE, B F 38 William 20
LOWERY, Daniel 3 38 Elizabeth
38 129 Geo 115 George W 6
George 42 114 115 123
Georgia A 38 James 6 38
115 128 Jock F 46 John H 46
Larken W 42 Larkin 129
Nancy 123 Thomas 6 42
LUPO, James M 110
MALAWIN, James 28
MALEDY, Nancy 131
MALERY, Mary 47
MALONE, Johnson 91
MANN, Manning H 63 Pinckney
83
MANNING, Elizabeth 29
Elizabeth A 146 Harriett 29
Harriett E 79 J C 146 156

James A 148 James Augustus
10 36 James C 10 60 61 67
87 102 146 148 Margaret J
36 152 Mary 32 Mary Ann B
83 Roland 29 79 W T 83 W
T H 71 86 William T H E 29
32 71 73 86 100 Wm T H 73
MARCH, H 104 Henry 93 127
128 137 133
MARSH, John 86
MARTIN, America 8 Austin 145
James 36 James A 36 Joicy
145 Martha 36 Netty 36 R C
75 Sarah 91 Thomas J 145
Wiley 36
MASON, C B 65 66 Comer B 65
Mary Ann 32
MASTERSON, John H 83 Louisa
39 Marshall 33 Mary Jane 33
39 99 Matilda 33 Matilda A
21 39
MATHEWS, Mary 65 Mary A 65
66
MATHIS, John T 16 Rebecca 20
Winfred Taylor 37
MATTHEW, John T 149
MATTHEWS, A J 140 146
Andrew T 106 F B 109 140
Francis B 109 James 32 105
106 149 John 51 106 109
146 149 John O 120 John T
112 120 149 150 Joseph B
86 Robert 129 T B 112 T E
134 Thomas E 134
MATTOX, Isabella 36 Isabella A
36 152 William B 36 125
William G 8
MAY, Benjamin 28 55 Catherine
53 Catherine Guice 28 Daniel

28 Henry 28 James F 28 John
28 P 65 Phillip 28 55 56 65 R
98 Stephen D 28 William 28
53 William D 28
MAYER, Louis 104
MAYES, G 133 J C 120 M D 97
109
MAYO, W R 89
MAYS, G W 61 Isaac C 28 61 M
D 111
MCADAMS, James F 20
MCBRIDE, Archibald 49
MCBROOM, James H 160
MCCALEB, W B 103 William B
103
MCCASKEY, John 74 75 136
MCCLELLAND, Benjamin 126
127 Benjamin M 126 Ellen 6
39 137 F C 128 Frances 128
Francis 40 Frederick M 126
127 James M 39 40
MCCLENDON, F W 157
MCCOMMAC, Alvin 61 Alvin W
61
MCCORMICK, A W 34 160
Alvin W 46 Benjamin 38
Catherine M 38 145 Emily A
140 Francis 10 38 140 141
145 Francis M 141 George L
38 Julia A 38 Thomas 144
Wm B 151
MCCOWN, Daniel 28 James 9 28
MCDANIEL, C C 17
MCDONALD, Donald 73
MCDUFFIE, A D 152 Archibald
D 8 36 William 13
MCFADIN, James 21 Jane A 128
T M 93 Thomas M 130

MCFARLAND, A 11 58 61 90
97 Malcomb 96 97 W 120 W
A 90 124 W H 86
MCFENNER, Sherard 74
MCGEE, F E 139
MCGILL, Stephen 59
MCGOUGH, Elizabeth 43
Elizabeth Burford 37 Frances
Jane 43 James P 150 Joseph
R 16 43 Josephus 148 158
Robert 69 W S 37 86 157
161 162 William H 18
William S 43
MCGRANE, J V 105
MCHATTON, James A 75
MCKEEN, A C 141 Alfred C 141
MCLAINE, Horatio 125
MCLAUGHLIN, Charles 51
MCLAURIN, D K 33 John D 33
MCMERTY, John 152
MCNAUGHTON, D 8
MCVICKER, P H 162
MEADOWS, Mary 70 Rawson
70
MEARS, Charles 116
MERRELL, A 161
MERRILL, William 86
MEYER, G 135 Gabriel 137
MIDDLETON, A 71
MILBURN, J E 148 Williamson
86
MILLER, Elijah 95 119 Elijah W
117 Fielding 59 76 77
MILLS, Jemus 111
MILNER , E R 95 Mary 124 U R
116 124 Uriel R 116 Wm A
105
MIMS, M W 137 Martin 67 68
81 85 Mary W 137 R L C 41

Robert L 147 S D 101 137 S
D Jr 41 S David 41 137 147
MITCHELL, J F 7 John B 8 139
Walter D 158
MIXON, Noel 48 Mary Ann 131
Noel 48
MOBLEY, Mary 7
MONTGOMERY, James 14
Samuel 95 118
MOOR, Henry 153
MOORE, B 99 Elizabeth Jane
Cook 139 George W 5 James
24 91 94 96 108 113 Jas 94
P T 3 Thomas J 3 Thomas L
76 William 7 William C 139
MORE, Matthew R 76
MORGAN, G M 140 George M
130
MORRIS, D 10 James 130
Permelia 33 Phillip 147
MORRISON, D C 84 J T 131
140
MORROW, Alabama 42 Charles
42 Joseph H 7 42 Nancy 42
William 42
MURPHEY, George R 118
MURPHY, G W 4 108 Geo W 95
MUSE, Henry B 14
MYERS, M D 110
NALL, James M 78
NELSON, Ashley 17 Ashley S 36
Nancy Ann Matilda 36
NEWTON, Isaac 90
NICHOLS, John 114
NIXON, R 53
NOLAN, David 164
NOLEN, John 157
NORMAN, Armstead 29 C L 68
117 C Y 120 Calvin 29

Calvin Y 119 Coatney L 85
Colvin Y 85 Courtney 29
Courtney L 22 38 F M 108
116 Frances 29 Lavina 29
Martha H 38 Martha A
Edwards 119 Sarah 29
Sylvester 29
NORRIS, Amanda 106 164 J J
139 John E 6 William S 9
NORSWORTHY, John 74
Thomas 53 W B 93
O'NEAL, Michael 53
ODOM, B W 111 Elizabeth 45
Jesse 15 Jesse 84 John 13 29
32 45 71 74 100 106 111
148 Pinkney 20 38 80 101
148
OLIVER, W J 163 William
142-143
OWEN, Eli 78
OWENS, Eli 19
PACE, James 66
PARDUE, Joseph 14
PARKER, Andrew 30 Asa 32 E
23 Elisha 32 J R 85 90 John
30 49 John R 89 Joseph R 43
Josiah 82 Sally 32 Sarah 30
William 32 William C 132
PARKEY, W H 64
PARKS, William A 136
PARROT, William 103
PARSONS, G 117
PATTERSON, A 17 Argus 136
John H 136
PATTON, James 118 James L
101 N M 128 William 5
PAYNE, William J 58 Daniel 33
Daniel 33 46 48 63 74 76 98
111 113 127 Daniel M 149

David 73 Dorothy 33 H 87
Mary A 48 Samuel 123 124
W J 58 63 W L 28 William J
51 75 Wm J 63
PEARSON, Davis 31 Eleanor 31
Jesse 32 Jesse E 14 Moses
31 62 65 Thomas 4 86 Thos
86 William 21 32 164
PEAVY, Hiram 128
PECK, Thomas J 85
PEEVEY, Hiram 92
PELAU, Robert 92
PERRY, S H 125 Samuel H 125
PETERSEN, B H 100
PETTIPAW, Everett 94
PETTIT, James 96 James 93
Arrena 89 James 68
PHELPS, Franklin A 150 Henry
81 93 100 101 John 15 112
163 Rebecca P 101
PHILLIPS, Charles W 82 David
A 92 100 S W 22 141 Silas
32 93 Silas W 141
PICKEL, W J 110 Washington J
95
PICKLE, W J 21
PILGREEN, Thomas 157
PINKARD, J M 7
PINKSTON, Milton 62 77
PIPES, William 11 68 134 Wm
134
PISTOLE, A 16
PLEASANT, R G 95 123 127
160 Ruffiin G 5 Ruffin
Goldston 123
PLEASANTS, R G 163
PLUMMER, Earnest 39 Gabriel
R 39 42 155 Jone (sic) 39

PLYANT, A E 119 131 Amanda
    Elizabeth 131 Elizabeth A
    155 Henry 4 131 155
POOL, Harrison 83 J H 87
POOLE, E E 156
POOR, M B H 118 Peggy 60
POPE, John W 47
POST, D C M 17
POWELL, Ann 80 C T 23 134 E
    Ann 96 James A 79 James M
    79 L M 23 Lewis M 134
    Solomon 80 96 110 115
PRATT, John 70
PRESLEY, Calvin 119
PRESTIDGE, J E 135
PRUITT, Peter 50 54
PUCKET, D 92 Daniel 100
PUCKETT, D 98 101 103 Daniel
    102 E R 21
PULLUM, Richard C 3
QUILLING, D H 76 D K 78
RABON, D 15 Frank 14 John 15
    Louis 20 William 15
RABUN, David 83 163 R F 55
    William 133 Wm 134
RAILY, Charles C 11
RAINS, F 104 Frederick 92 T A
    92 103 Thomas A 92
RAKEY, C H 52 Charles H 46 60
    Charles N 47 J N 61 John 55
    61 Sarah Ann 120
RAMSEY, C L 96 D B 58 96 97
    G W 96 97 H W 96 97
    Humphrey W R 97 J W 131
    James 52 96 97 John 96 97 L
    W 96 97 Martha Ann 76
    Mary 96 S W 111 115 126
    135 Simpson W 12 29 76
    115 Wilkes 86 96

RANEY, M J 116 W J 103
    William 56
RATCLIFF, B F 125
RATLIFF , T T 89 Thomas T 46
    59 72 89
RAY, John 48 57 58
RAYBURN, David 130 Davis
    130
REDDEN, David 4
REED, G W 126
REGENBERG, H 88 106 126
REGENBURG, H 63 65-67 85
    87 89 91 93 100-102 104
    116 129 136 138 148 149
    156 157 Henry 13 33 81 87
    91 124 129 136
REPHART, George 69 George
    W 69
REPOND, Elizabeth Cabray 156
REPPOND, E A 132 159
    Elizabeth 159 L C 23 Lewis
    112
RESTER, Albert Hezekiah 103
    Daniel Frederick 103 Francis
    Marion 103 Gideon 103
    Hezekiah 103 Liberty 103
    Mary Jane 103 Sarah 103
    William 103
REYNOLDS, Eily A 140 G W 10
    72 George W 72 140 James
    C 164 W M 111
RICHARDSON, Clementine H
    27 Robert N 95 Robert W 54
    Robertson 119
RIMES, B M 102 B W 102
    Cinderella 32 Francis L 32
    John D 32 93 Louisa C 32 93
    Thomas W 32 William L 32
RIORDAN, Evaline 73

ROAN, James 55 P 108
ROANE, James 56 78
ROBB, Abel 22
ROBERTS, Joseph F 70 J T 113
    James F 123 John T 84 113
    123 Joseph F 70 Mary 71
    Mary P 71 R R 9 William 52
    54
ROBERTSON, John 56 John B
    24 136 John V 52 57 74
ROBINSON, George 153 George
    W 135 J B L 16 James 79
    Jared 79 144 148 149 Jarred
    144 John B 99 S L 23
    Samuel L 118 Thomas 5
ROGERS, John 33 48 122
ROPER, Lou 164
ROSS, James 137 James R 147
    John A 163 164 Wm E 137
ROSSITER, E A 38 131 Eliza A
    162 Eliza Ann 107 108 131
    Elizabeth Ann 40 162
    George 12 40 162 George M
    M 40 162 Harriett D 40
    Jefferson B 40 162 W H 108
ROWLAND, L F 133 Lucien F
    34 Sallie H 133
RUNNELLS, G P 9 J C 20
RUSH, Louis 8
RUSSELL, E C 97 James 103
SANDERS, J B 140 145
SAPITER, Robert 71
SAVAGE, George M 30 60 75
SAWYER, Daniel 119 James J
    119 Thomas 48 Willis 119
SCARBOROUGH, Lawrence 49
    Sarahe 49
SCOTT, J W 141 John W 145
    154

SEALE, James 48 49 James A 57
    James H 53 Joseph Brent 82
    Joshua 82 Lewis P 82
SEALS, Thomas 11
SELLERS, Thomas 10
SESSIONS, J G 154
SEWEL, James H 83
SHACKELFORD, P J 3
SHANNON, William 91
SHAW, D 22 Daniel 42 155
    Joseph 4
SHELTON, Lewis N 50
SHEPHERD, James B 33 S 94
    114 115 Sylvanus 33 104
    105 114 118 160
SHEPPARD, Benjamin D 142 J
    B 15 S 118 Wright Jr 158
SHIELDS, John 12
SHLENKER, Alex 93 104 106
    115 121 127 Alexander 104
    133 137 J 12 Jacob 128 148
SHOLARS, O B 158
SHORES, John C 73
SHORT, J B 15
SIMMONS, James 164 M F 156
    M T 15
SIMPSON, Thomas 120
SIMS, Benjamin 55 56 G W 73
    88 98 113 144 145 George
    W 12 91 113 145 R J 22
SIPES, William 48
SKAINS, Flora Ann 116 120
    Thomas N 120
SLAWSON, James D 105
SLED, E D 134 149 158
    Etheldred 142 149
SLOAN, Permelia 43
SLOANE, W H 127
SLONE, William 127

179

SMITH , Cassandra 83 William C 72 78 94 135 140 143-146 152 156 157 160 Wm C 136 149 A 143 Adeline 68 B F 162 Banks A 83 Benjamin 141 Benjamin F 141 C M 60 61 69 138 Cassandra 74 100 Casandra L 89 107 Claiborne 67 Claiborne M 73 Claiborne M 60 E B 157 Elizabeth A 146 Frances J 40 Joel 126 127 137 John 64 77 132 John P 82 John T 23 Luke 74 83 Luke H 74 89 Nancy C 3 Nancy C Bennett 138 Obadiah 82 Oliver P 164 S N 94 Sally A 157 Saml 159 Samuel 93 132 Samuel A 83 T M 123 159 Thomas 124 Thomas M 76 145 159 Thomas Mercer 145 Thomas W 27 W C 107 113 114 117 119 122 131 152 W J 9 22 W P 5 William C 47 59 62 64 65 107 112 113 114 117 118 122 123 125129 132 136 138 146 147-149 151 164 William Claiborne 13 William P 157 Wm C 73 112 121 123 127 129 145 158 161 162 164

SPEARS, W L 124 127

SPELLERS, H C 10

SPENCER, J M 22

SQUIRES, George W 82

STANBACK, R 151

STANLEY, Nancy 10 34 Nancy E Stewart 34

STANSELL, Allen 111

STANSIL, A 18

STEADLEY, James J 65

STEEL, John 18 80 Samuel B 80

STEEN, E 50 Elias 50

STERLING, John 97 98 Rachel 28

STEWART, David 12 92 David G 34 Elizabeth 119 George D 131 155 Jonathan B 34 Mary 60 Mary L 14 34 Mary Louise 60 Robert 155 T J 22 Thomas J 60 85 101 136 137 Washington W 34

STINSON, G A 143 George A 8 139 Joseph 116 Mary 116

STOCKS, John G 146 159

STOW, John 92 139

STRINGER, J A 22

STRIPLING, Arthur 24 37 161 E 23 G W 161 George W 37 J S 23

STROOP, James 60 James G 85

SUPO, James M 141

SUTTON, James D 35 James S 4 John S 35 Sara Jane 35 William 35

TABOR, Elijah 62 97 155 George W 4 40 John Burrell 40 Mary W Edmonds 40 Robert 155

TATE, W C 46 Elizabeth 138 James M 7 Sarah Ann Wright 42 T J 24

TAY, John E 108

TAYLOR, A M 146 Alex M 51 63 69 105 152 157 158 Alexander 50 157 Alexander M 18 37 101 127 158 Ann 87 Elias 9 143 Elizabeth 43

H 89 J A 99 J G 18 92 104
107 132 149 J G Jr 158
James 164 James A 99 127
James K 51 John 19 21
45-50 52-56 62 106 119 139
142 157 164 John H 127
Jordan 21 Jordan G 96 133
157 158 Jourdan G 54 Nancy
15 Robert G 136 Saml W
152 Samuel W 152 Sarah 18
William 106 152
TELFORD, J 140 James A 84
Joseph 149
TEMPLE, D G 112 139 David G
139 Martha 156 William 156
TERRELL, Virginia C 133 W S
133
TERRY, J M 19 Joseph M 85
Joseph W 87 145
THACKER, Isaac R 56
THEOBALDS, W P 57
THOMAS, A 157 Asa 90 102
161 B B 23 155 J W 121
John W 121 140 Liberty K
14 38 81 98 116 143 S B 21
Sampson B 61
THOMPKINS, Sarah 161
THOMPSON, Angeline 53 Anna
81 Arrena 81 93 Charles 123
Charles J 123 George 114 J
L 140 J R 35 150 John M
114 L C 140 R E 140 T S 13
Valinda 61 W B 81 William
63 64 74 80 114 116 William
B 93 William T 20 Wm 138
TIDWELL, John T 9
TIGNOR, Anna 142 H J 142
TISDALE, W T 94
TODD, W W 112

TOLER, William H 164
TOMLINSON, J E 68 John E 68
TRAILER, John 21 S E 21
TRAYLOR, Emily L 27 J C 78 J
H 101 J M 69 James M 69
James M 69 James M 79
John 60 76 101 Josiah 76
Josiah C 29 60 69 75 P B 78
79 101 Paschal B 101
Samuel 79 Sarah 60 76
TREMBLE, J E 13
TROUSDALE, D B 97 99 David
B 92 97
TUBB, B M 112 Benj 143
Benjamin 5 Benjamin M 15
81 82 Elizabeth 38 G W 62
Geo 143 George 15 143 144
George W 90 91 H M 96
Harriett 6 J B 144 Jesse 118
144 John B 5 38 R 82 R F 62
William 5 38
TUCKER, D J 23 Daniel J 115
TURNER, Henry C 77 87 J M
117 144 James M 22 47 77
87 Mary 33
UNDERWOOD, Ann 73 J M 102
113 149 James M 12 35 113
149 James W 150 Sarah 102
W 61 64 67 102 Wiley 55 58
64 94 95 102
VAN HOOK, Allen 37 Charity 37
I A R 51 89 90 92 100 Isaac
A R 52 Jackson 37 Maria E
36 Mary 36 Martha J 89
Martha Jane Wood 90
Thomas 36 51 52 54 55 58
59 72 76 86 88 91 100 105
131 Wade 37 64 65 67 69 84
Thos 69 88 107 123

VANEYHAM, William H 56
VINES, David 13 J W 12 Nealy
20 Nelia 159
WADE, A 3 Absolom 161 James
L 161 James Thomas 3
WALKER, Alexander 58 J W 22
W W 23 151 Wesley W 151
WALL, Reuben 154
WALLACE, Elizabeth 142 143 J
B 80 W B 11 143 William B
142
WALLAS, W A 23
WALLIS, James 23
WARD, David 19 52 109 129
Davis 111 E H 150 Elisha
109 Mary P 33 118
WARE, George N 63
WARREN, Jasper 98 Joseph M
98 Joseph W 98 Sarah 98
WASOM, W M 15
WASSEN, W W 112
WASSON, W W 113 William W
113
WATERS, Amanda J 40
WATKINS, James 108 113 John
S 16
WATSON, Thomas J 145 W A
75 W W 50
WATTERS, Armand D 162 H B
117
WEAVER, John 86
WEBB, Harriett 40 Harriett D
162 Robert 67 Robert C 53
68 Robert C Jr 40 107
WEBSTER, Y O S 160
WEIL, M 138
WELDEN, John 3
WEST, B B 63 83 84 86-88 91
106 107 121 126 Ben B 87

Benjamin B 72 86 114 126
Benjamin W 87 Benjamin
114 Catherine 41 Elizabeth N
121 John 35 150 Lizzie N
121
WESTBROOKS, Uriah 65
WHEELIS, S T 146
WHITE, J A 112 J C B 4 John M
16 Nicholas F 90 S W 60
Wiley 8 William 9 95 132
WHITING, H E 112 Harrison E
112
WHITSON, E 81 E B 85 86
Enoch B 85
WICKLIFF, Joseph A 126 127
WIEL, M 141
WIGGINS, J C 143
WILHITE, P 10 Philemon 51 T
140 T J 121 Thomas 51
Thomas J 28 51 64 William
28 William J 9
WILLIAMS, Eliza 6 Elizabeth 62
F B 153 Frank 82 Isaac 20
Israel B 120 130 J T 84 J W
110 James M 17 Job M 34
John 9 120 153 John C 35
Josiah T 84 Narcissa Eliza
130 Narcissa Elizabeth 130
Rachel C 34 Richard B 118
Rosetta 153
WILLSON, J H 65 72 77 James
H 52 72 77 Jesse 62 John H
52 John L 65 Permilia 52
Permilia Jones 52 Robert J
155
WILSON, Hiram A 43 James B
43 144 Thomas A 48
Victoria A 43 William 74 75

WINDES, E B 78 131-133 139
142 Edward B 13 30 41 57
58 62 63 78 Elizabeth 41 O
H P 57 Oliver H P 30 75 R
W 73 111 141 Robert W 30
57 73 Saml 57 Saml P 58
Samuel P 57
WINN, Margaret 160
WISE, Caroline L 68
WOMACK, John B 143
WOOD, Abosolem 89 Amanda E
110 Amanda Elizabeth Jane
110 Jenetta 110 John 110
John W 21 Mary A 43
Matthew 48 Purvis 91 92
Willis 46 54 56 120
WOODARD, J E 10
WOOLEY, W A 18
WOOSLEY, James 55
WRIGHT, D M 6 138 152 164 J
G 106 138 164 J W 7 John
42 106 138 John E 42 John
G Jr 6 John G Sr 6 John H
109 115 Owen 42 S L 138
Samuel L 85 138 Sarah Ann
42 Thomas H 7 Thomas M
106 Thomas R 42
YONGUE, Delaware S 113
Delaware S Jones 43 H 93
106 107 Hugh 106 Hugh 43
89 92 93 107 113
YOUNG, John 92

Index
Slaves

Slaves, Full Names

COWAN, Duncan M 64
HARRISON, John 62
JENKINS, George 62
MORRISON, Winney A 32

NORTH, Peter 31
TALBOT, John 158
WATERS, Henry 134

Slaves
First Names Only

Aaron 28 33 37 41 65
Abe 37 41 154
Abel 102
Abley 39
Abner 29
Abraham 42
Abram 29 33 34 94 116
Abrom 70
Adaline 34
Adam 62 109 147
Addison 73
Adeline 32
Affrey 92
Aggy, Little 33
Agnes 37
Ailsey 38
Albert 40 130 163 Prince 31
Alcy 30
Aleck 35 88 96
Alex 27 32 53
Alexander 30 64 123
Aley 147
Alfred 30 31 39 41 43 77 154
Alfrey 43

Alice 39 43
Alick 155
Allen 31 32 71 96 112 119 120
      154
Allick 136
Ally 95
Alsey 28
Alson 154
Alvin 37
Aly 38
Amanda 36-40 42 58 141 144
      157
Amos 116 159
Amy 37 124
Anderson 34 37 54 89 99 147
Andrew 41 51 131
Andy 29 33 39 42 57 102 104
      108 111 112 116 117 129
      159
Angelina 34
Angeline 39 128 159
Ann 27 28 36-41 52 66 93 97 105
      107 119 127 137 143 148
      151 153 154 159 162 Big 71

Georgy 72 Julian 122 July 52
Mary 31 34 71 149 158 Milly
147 Sarah 29 135 139
Anna 94
Anne 136 141
Anney 72
Anthony 38 55 119
Antony 95
Arch 41
Aron 39
Arrina 139
Arthur 28
Ashack 42
Audry 47
Augustus 135
Austin 141
Avery 143
Barbery 113
Becca 147
Beck 70
Becky 43
Bedford 31
Ben 36 37 39 42 85 94 113 141
153 157
Benjamin 37 43
Benny 157
Benton 41
Berry 157
Beth 40
Bets 83
Betsey 34 94 101 102
Betsy 43 47 70 71 145
Bett 162
Betty 33 40 63 68 69 90 105
Bicea 36 39 78
Big Ann 71
Big Martin 71
Big Rachel 31
Big Sally 29

Biley 113
Bill 27 30 39 41 42 44 73 85 89
93 100 122 124
Bina 96
Bird 39 142 164
Bittie 42
Bitty 33
Bob 31 36 37 39 42 46 48 89 123
144 151 154 155 157
Bolliver 111
Booker 123
Buck 37 69
Bud 69
Bunch 94
Burell 40
Burr 27
Burrel 162
Burton 149
Cacey 39
Caesar 95
Caleb 63 93
Camelia 147
Candis 107 161
Cargel 55
Caroline 30 31 33-36 39 41-43 45
47 62 64 65 70 72 74 78 81
84 89 96 98 110 117 122
140 144 147 149 150
Caswell 80
Catherine 29 33 98 102 113 123
133 148
Ceasor 136
Ceasor 31
Cela 95
Celia 27 38 153
Celler 41
Cely 110
Cenia 42
Chana 124

Chaney 42
Chany 28 29 30 35 39 110
Charity 27 28 30 37 39 50 70 80
    81 101 105 121 129 161
Charles 28 29 32 38 40 41 48 50
    52 55 67 73 74 76 94 95 102
    111 138 145 154 162
Charley 37 42 157 164
Charlie 41
Charlo 31
Charlott 40 112 159
Charlotte 30 34 37 51 75 99 109
    132 139
Charlotte Elizabeth 105
Charly 70
Chase 34
Chastity 28
Cheny 73
Cherry 85
Chesby 94
Cinderella 124
Cindy 119
Cinna 30
Cipio 31
Clara 42 95 126 138
Clarea 38
Clarissa 28 155
Clarissy 143
Clarisy 157
Clark 112
Clarrissa 161
Clinsa 37 42
Clow 119
Cloy 31
Colara 37
Columbus 141
Cook 37 157
Cordelia 114 116
Corene 148

Corissee 144
Cory 71
Crease 35
Cyndy 28
Cynthia 29 34 42 155
Dalilah 144
Dan 31
Dandrige 28
Daniel 31 36 38 72 94 101 134
Darcas 39
Dave, Little 30
Dave, Old 30
Dave 28
David 59 127 137 154 164
Davis 109
Davis 94
Dearing 42
Delcey 28
Delia 41 84
Delila 29
Delilah 131 133 144
Delphey 28
Dely 36
Dennis 28 42
Derry 31
Desoto 43
Diana 129
Dianah 138
Dianah 154
Dianna 94 105 139
Diannah 28 42
Dinah 42
Dick 30 31 37 38 42 67 94 109
    123 135
Dicy 32 139 151
Dilcy 34 76
Dilley 43
Dinah/Diannah 42
Dinah 33 85 148

Nicey 28 123
Nicy 55 72 128
Noah 35 121 156
Nolia 30
North 29
Novel 52
Old Dave 30
Old Phillip 31
Olive 138
Oliver 45 48
Olivia 49
Olly 35 163
Orleana 39
Palina 102
Parthena 85
Parthenia 37 38
Patience 31 38 39 96
Patrick 59
Patsey 41 46 59 65
Patty 39
Paul 38
Pegge 31
Peggy 27 31-33 59 70 129 154
Penelope 28
Penney 104
Penny 37 50 57 124
Perliney 73
Perry 111
Peter 28 29 34 38 42 55 71 85 97
    103 106 108 122 124 143
    144 155 157 163
Pharoah 153
Pheba 107
Phebe 38 67
Phebia 71
Pheby 67
Pherese 116
Phil 71 81
Philip 29 53

Philip, Old 31
Phill 56 68 88 90
Phillip 31 94
Phillis 30 32 87 97 147
Phronia 144
Pink 92
Pinney 107
Pleasant 96 123
Polly 66 84 94 112 149 151 153
Pompy 41
Porter 27 29
Primas 31
Primus 139
Prince 65 90 111
Prince Albert 31
Priss 31 94
Prissilla 83 92
Quincy 111
Quint 132
Rachel 27 30 32 35-38 42 50 86
    93 94 96 115 141 150 Big
    31
Rachiel 128
Ralph 123
Randal 36 59
Randall 152
Raney 31
Rassette 43
Reddico 137
Reuben 28 39 42 155
Revs 40 162
Rhoda 122
Rhodo 30
Richard 134
Ringo 34
Roan 39
Robb 27
Robert 35 51 119 146 149
Rocky 41

Rolly 57
Ropetta 38
Rose 31 32 40 42 54 96 107 120
    130 162 Little 71
Rosean 50 74
Ross 41
Rossette 94
Ruben 40
Rudy 138 157
Rufus 131 138 160
Ruth 94
Ruthy 141
Sabre 37
Salina 125
Salley 55
Sallie 41 154
Sally, Big 29 Little 29
Sally 32 34 35 37 40 61 73 77
    129 150 157
Sam 30 31 32 37 42 66 94 96 108
    125 138 141 160 162
Sampson 32
Samuel 98 113 141
Sandford 133 142
Sandy 35 37 42 94
Sara 108 154
Sarah 27 28 32 34 35 38 41-43
    46 53 54 61 66 67 71 77 82
    87 94 96 131 138 142 155
    156 158
Sarah Ann 29 135 139
Sawyer 31
Sealy 29
Selph 62
Selvey 31
Sermantha 34
Setta 43
Shaddeus 133
Shaddeuz 136

Shadrach 27
Shadrick 107 126
Sharlett 127
Sharlot 79
Sharlott 93
Sharper 32 52
Shedrick 70
Shelby 76
Shelly 60
Shilla 147
Sidney 157
Silas 39 42 99 153 155
Silla 130
Silva, Little 31
Silver 138
Silvey 94 154
Simon 28 89 147
Sinday 161
Sine 159
Sing 27
Sipp 38
Solomon 33 56 84 91 94 123
Sopha 110
Sophia 27 39 124 157
Spencer 41 142
Spincer 164
Squier 119
Squire 42
Stephen 29 30 34 37 41 60 70 76
    92 94 98 100 144 150 153
Stepney 92 94
Sterling 153
Steve 107 159
Steven 155
Stipney 31
Sukey 29
Sump 94
Sun 27

www.ingramcontent.com/pod-product-compliance
Lightning Source LLC
Chambersburg PA
CBHW072225270326
41930CB00010B/2003